The New Face of Mexican Migration

The New Face of Mexican Migration: A Transnational Community in Yucatán and California

Edited by Wayne A. Cornelius, Micah Gell-Redman, Hillary S. Kosnac, Pedro Lewin-Fischer, and Verónica Noriega

Center for Comparative Immigration Studies
University of California, San Diego
9500 Gilman Drive MC 0548
La Jolla, CA 92093
(858) 822- 4447

Printed in the United States of America

Cover design by Bret Silvis.
Cover photograph by Debra A. Cornelius.

ISBN 1519767862   (paper)

Procession through Tunkás, Yucatán, during the town's annual fiesta, 2015.

(Photo by Carlos León)

The New Face
of Mexican Migration

A Transnational Community in Yucatán and California

edited by

Wayne A. Cornelius
Micah Gell-Redman
Hillary S. Kosnac
Pedro Lewin-Fischer
Verónica Noriega

La Jolla, California

Center for Comparative Immigration Studies
University of California, San Diego
2016

BOOKS AND SPECIAL JOURNAL ISSUES BASED ON RESEARCH CONDUCTED BY THE MEXICAN MIGRATION FIELD RESEARCH AND TRAINING PROGRAM AT THE UNIVERSITY OF CALIFORNIA-SAN DIEGO[1]

2007: *Impacts of Border Enforcement on Mexican Migration: The View from Sending Communities*, eds. Wayne A. Cornelius and Jessa M. Lewis. La Jolla, CA and Boulder, CO: Center for Comparative Immigration Studies, UCSD, and Lynne Rienner Publishers.

2007: *Mayan Journeys: The New Migration from Yucatán to the United States*, eds. Wayne A. Cornelius, David S. FitzGerald, and Pedro Lewin-Fischer. La Jolla, CA and Boulder, CO: Center for Comparative Immigration Studies, UCSD, and Lynne Rienner Publishers.

2008: *Caminantes del Mayab: Los nuevos migrantes de Yucatán a los Estados Unidos*, eds. Wayne A. Cornelius, David S. FitzGerald, y Pedro Lewin-Fischer. Mérida, Yuc., and México, DF: Instituto de Cultura de Yucatán/Instituto Nacional de Antropología e Historia.

2009: *Four Generations of Norteños: New Research from the Cradle of Mexican Migration*, eds. Wayne A. Cornelius, David S. FitzGerald, and Scott Borger. La Jolla, CA and Boulder, CO: Center for Comparative Immigration Studies, UCSD, and Lynne Rienner Publishers.

2009: *Migration from the Mexican Mixteca: A Transnational Community in Oaxaca and California*, eds. Wayne A. Cornelius, David S. FitzGerald, Jorge Hernández-Díaz, and Scott Borger. La Jolla, CA and Boulder, CO: Center for Comparative Immigration Studies, UCSD, and Lynne Rienner Publishers.

2010: *Mexican Migration and the U.S. Economic Crisis: A Transnational Perspective*, eds. Wayne A. Cornelius, David S. FitzGerald, Pedro Lewin-Fischer, and Leah Muse-Orlinoff. La Jolla, CA and Boulder, CO: Center for Comparative Immigration Studies, UCSD, and Lynne Rienner Publishers.

2011: *Migración desde la Mixteca: Una comunidad transnacional en Oaxaca y California*, eds. Wayne A. Cornelius, David S. FitzGerald, Jorge Hernández-Díaz, y Scott Borger. México, D.F.: Miguel Ángel Porrúa/Universidad Autónoma Benito Juárez de Oaxaca/Center for Comparative Immigration Studies, University of California-San Diego.

---

[1] All books are available through Amazon.com. The special journal issue can be downloaded at: http://link.springer.com/journal/10903/16/3/page/1

2011: *Recession Without Borders: Mexican Migrants Confront the Economic Downturn,* eds. David S. Fitzgerald, Rafael Alarcón, and Leah Muse-Orlinoff. La Jolla, CA and Boulder, CO: Center for Comparative Immigration Studies, UCSD, and Lynne Rienner Publishers.

2013: *The Wall Between Us: A Mixteco Migrant Community in Mexico and the United States,* eds. David S. FitzGerald, Jorge Hernández Díaz, and David Keyes. La Jolla, CA: Center for Comparative Immigration Studies, UCSD.

2013: *Return Migration, Health, and Sexuality in a Transnational Mexican Community,* eds. Wayne A. Cornelius, Alejandra Lizardi-Gómez, Allison Van Vooren, and David Keyes. La Jolla, CA, and Guadalajara, Jalisco: Center for Comparative Immigration Studies, UCSD, and Universidad de Guadalajara.

2014: "Special Topics in Immigrant Health: The Health of Indigenous Mayan Migrants from Yucatán, México," ed. María Luisa Zúñiga. Collection of four articles in *Journal of Immigrant and Minority Health,* 16(3): 329-64 (June).

2015: *One Step In and One Step Out: The Lived Experience of Immigrant Participants in the Deferred Action for Childhood Arrivals (DACA) Program,* eds. Hillary S. Kosnac, Wayne A. Cornelius, Tom K. Wong, Micah Gell-Redman, and D. Alex Hughes. La Jolla, CA: Center for Comparative Immigration Studies, UCSD.

2016: *The New Face of Mexican Migration: A Transnational Community in Yucatán and California,* eds. Wayne A. Cornelius, Micah Gell-Redman, Hillary S. Kosnac, Pedro Lewin-Fischer, and Verónica Noriega. La Jolla, CA: Center for Comparative Immigration Studies, UCSD.

CONTENTS

Young folkloric dancers prepare to perform in Tunkás' annual fiesta.

(Photo by Carlos León)

Preface

WAYNE A. CORNELIUS

This volume is the fourteenth in a series of books and special journal issues that have been based on fieldwork conducted by the Mexican Migration Field Research and Training Program (MMFRP), a program of the Center for Comparative Immigration Studies at the University of California-San Diego (see the preceding pages for full citations).

Since it was established in 2004, the MMFRP's *modus operandi* has been simple: Dig deep in a small number of research sites, return to them often, conduct highly detailed in-home interviews, and follow migrants to their U.S. destinations. We have sought to document and explain changes in migration and U.S. settlement behaviors, as well as their consequences for health, education, labor market participation, civic engagement, and family life. This was accomplished by studying, in great depth, the same set of three rural, high-emigration communities, located in the states of Jalisco, Oaxaca, and Yucatán,[2] and their principal U.S. satellite communities. Both sending and receiving communities have been restudied at three-year intervals. Thus, the MMFRP has had a quasi-longitudinal research design, in which the population interviewed overlapped substantially with participants in the preceding field study. For example, in the 2015 field study in Tunkás, Yucatán and southern California, 43 percent of survey respondents had also been interviewed in our previous (2012) survey of Tunkaseños. Working collaboratively with students and faculty in Mexican partner institutions, we collected field data consecutively in the Mexican and U.S. research sites, usually during the January-March period, using a multi-method approach that included standardized survey interviews, semi-structured qualitative interviews, and ethnographic observation.

The MMFRP's primary research sites in Mexico were purposively selected to maximize variation in terms of economic development/poverty level (they are classified by Mexico's National Population Council as low-, medium-, and high-marginality municipios), ethnic composition (one mestizo, two indigenous—Maya and Mixteco), density and longevity of U.S.-bound migration experience (the proportion of residents with such experience ranges from 22.4 percent, in our Yucatán research site, to 70 percent, in the Jalisco

---

[2]A fourth migrant-sending community, located in the state of Zacatecas, was included only in the first MMFRP project.

site). All three migrant-sending communities are small towns, ranging from 1,264 to 2,812 inhabitants. The U.S. cities in which migrants from these towns have clustered include the San Francisco Bay area, Los Angeles, Anaheim, Santa Ana, and San Diego County in California, plus Oklahoma City, OK. In each year's MMFRP project a snowball sample of U.S.-based migrants originating in our Mexican research community has been interviewed, enabling us to study integration processes in the United States, return migration flows to the community of origin, and the impacts of U.S. immigration policies and programs like DACA (the Deferred Action for Childhood Arrivals program) that are of interest mainly to U.S. residents.

The substantive foci of MMFRP projects have varied considerably over the years, although there have been several constants -- most notably, the impacts of U.S. immigration laws and policies on individual-level migration and settlement behaviors. Each year's project explored at least one or two topics not previously addressed in detail in preceding MMFRP studies. Thus, we expanded our research agenda to include such subjects as the structure and functioning of the people-smuggling industry (*coyotaje*); effects of the U.S. Great Recession of 2007-2009 on migration to the United States, settlement in that country, and return migration to Mexico; impacts of sub-national U.S. immigration control policies on migration and settlement processes; policy innovations like the DACA program and the Border Patrol's "enhanced {legal] consequences" strategy to reduce recidivism among undocumented migrants; the influence of migration on nutrition, substance abuse, mental health, sexual and reproductive health; returned migrants' strategies for investing income earned in the United States; the process of "dissimilation" (how returning migrants become cultural outsiders in their own hometown); determinants of educational attainment, occupational health, and civic participation on both sides of the border; the impacts of social networks and new communication technologies on migration and transnational family life; how migration shapes ethnic identification and religiosity, and vice versa; how climate change in Mexico affects migration behavior; the interface between internal and international migration; and the decision to stay home in Mexico rather than migrate to the United States.

Hardly any of these additions to the MMFRP research agenda were foreseen when the program was launched twelve years ago. But we were attentive to changes in the binational research environment, and our research communities in Mexico and the United States proved to be excellent "living laboratories" for studying a broad range of social phenomena. The end result is a large body of fieldwork-based research that addresses, in highly detailed fashion, most (not all) elements of the Mexico-to-U.S. migration experience that are of interest to consumers and practitioners of scholarship in this area. In 2015-16 the MMFRP is continuing under new leadership, gathering data in new field research sites, exploring cutting-edge educational and public health issues related to Mexican migration.

DATA AND METHODS

The data for this volume are drawn from standardized, face-to-face survey interviews with 558 residents of Tunkás, Yucatán, and its satellite communities in the United States. These included three California cities: Inglewood (part of the Los Angeles metropolitan area), Anaheim, and Santa Ana. Survey interviews were supplemented with 87 semi-structured, qualitative interviews conducted in the same places. These interviews were digitally recorded and transcribed for analysis.

In preparation for the Tunkás-based survey, all 1,170 dwelling units in the town believed to be inhabited were canvassed in January 2015. The field team attempted to interview all persons aged 15-65 in each household if they had a strong connection with Tunkás, i.e., resided there, or had been born there, or had parents or grandparents had been residents of Tunkás. In addition, interviewees must have been able to speak Spanish or English (no interviews were conducted in the Maya language), and must have been able to provide informed consent. In the case of potential interviewees aged 15-17, consent was obtained from a parent or another adult in the house. Our sample includes some Tunkás-born persons who were no longer residents of Tunkás but were encountered visiting relatives during the town's annual fiesta, which coincided with our fieldwork. The same eligibility criteria applied to persons interviewed in southern California. As noted above, 43 percent of all survey respondents had also been interviewed in the previous (2012) MMFRP survey of Tunkaseños in Yucatán and California. All inhabited dwellings in Tunkás were visited at least once by our field interviewers, and in many cases all eligible household members were interviewed. Since we sought to interview the town's entire population between 15 and 65 years of age, there was no sampling procedure and therefore no sampling error.

For survey interviews with California-based Tunkaseños, a modified snowball sample was developed using contact information provided on a voluntary basis by family members interviewed in Tunkás. This contact information was supplemented by information from key informants in the communities of Tunkaseño migrants living in California. Potential interviewees were approached at their place of residence or at social gatherings of Tunkasenos that occurred during our California fieldwork.

Subjects for qualitative interviews were a subset of respondents to the standardized survey questionnaire administered in Tunkás and California. Qualitative interviewees were chosen non-randomly from survey interviewees who had demonstrated in-depth knowledge of the subjects to be explored through qualitative interviews. Like survey respondents, qualitative interviewees must have been born in Tunkás or were the offspring of persons born there. For the qualitative interviews conducted by our working group on migration and substance abuse, additional eligibility criteria were imposed, as described in Chapter 3 of this volume.

Our data collection instruments and interviewing protocols were reviewed and approved by the Human Research Protections Program at the University of California-San Diego. All interviewers were Spanish-fluent and had received at least four months of intensive training in quantitative and qualitative ieldwork methods, the ethics of field research, and human subject protections before fieldwork commenced. Joint training of San Diego-based and Yucatán-based field interviewers occurred at UC San Diego in November 2014. Using a 29-member field team, interviewing was conducted in Tunkás between January 25 and February 5, 2015 and in our southern California research sites from February 14 to March 10, 2015.

KEY FINDINGS

The MMFRP's fourth study of Tunkaseños in Yucatán and California took shape at a time when overall Mexican migration to the United States had plummeted to the 1970 level, as measured by U.S. Border Patrol apprehension statistics. Previous MMFRP studies in Tunkás had documented a similar trend, with the proportion of interviewees planning to migrate to the United States in the next twelve months falling from 16.8 percent in our 2006 survey of the town to 7.4 percent in 2009, and 4.6 percent in 2012. The steepest decline in intention to go north occurred between 2006 and 2009, precisely when the Great Recession was deepening in the United States. The same pattern was observed in the MMFRP's research communities in Jalisco and Oaxaca. Both Border Patrol apprehensions and migrants' remittances to relatives in Mexico (perhaps a leading indicator of migration flows) have been trending upward since 2014,[3] but new Mexico-to-U.S. migration remains far below pre-Great Recession levels. We hypothesized that the sharp contraction of north-bound migration flows since 2006 was largely a consequence of persisting, weak labor demand in the United States, stemming from the Great Recession. But what other factors may be influencing Mexicans to stay home? And, were potential migrants whose current plans do not include migration to the United States permanent stay-at-homes, or just people who have temporarily delayed

---

[3]For example, in August 2015, 13.1 percent more in family remittances flowed to Mexico than in the same month in 2014 (Li-Ng & Salgado-Torres, 2015). U.S. Border Patrol apprehensions in Fiscal Year 2014 totaled 486,651, a 16 percent increase over the previous year, but most of tbe increase was driven by a surge in unaccompanied child migrants from Central America (Krogsstad & Passel, 2014).

going north? Was there a "new calculus of staying home in Mexico" that had taken hold in communities of emigration like Tunkás?

The first MMFRP field study of Tunkaseños, in 2006, had devoted some attention to the non-migrating population (Castillo, et al., 2007), but that exploration was limited to individual-level factors that traditionally root people in their home community, such as advanced age, poor health, lack of financial resources, limited English, family obligations, and cultural practices. For our 2015 restudy we went beyond these traditional deterrents to mobility. We sought to examine the effects of macro-level variables such as changing U.S. immigration enforcement practices, improving labor market conditions in Mexico, changes in the people-smuggling industry that might have increased risk to migrants, an upsurge in organized crime activities in the borderlands, and accelerated family reunification on the U.S. side of the border, partly a function of tighter U.S. border enforcement.

As reported in Chapter 1, we found that just 2.5 percent of our Tunkás-based interviewees intended to migrate to the United States in the following twelve months – a further decline from our 2012 survey. But we found no single-factor explanation for the higher incidence of stay-at-homes. There was a significant residue of the Great Recession, in the form of a perception that finding employment in the United States was much more difficult now than before the Recession. But the only statistically significant, U.S. policy-related variable was the belief/perception that deportations from the United States had risen sharply in the last five years. Moreover, Tunkasenos who held this belief were actually *more* likely to migrate to the United States than those who were less well-informed about the large-scale deportations occurring under the Obama administration. While other non-traditional determinants of decisions to stay home were influential in the expected direction (especially awareness of organized migrant-kidnapping activities in the borderlands), they were not significant predictors in our multivariate models.

There were some important negative findings. For example, while people-smugglers are now more likely to be perceived as being involved with criminal organizations, this perception was not discouraging migration because the *polleros* used by Tunkasenos continued to have an extremely good track record of meeting their clients' needs and not abusing them. Family ties were the single most important reason why people stay in Tunkás, but family connectivity was also a powerful motivator of international migration. The number of U.S.-based relatives proved to be the strongest predictor of propensity to migrate to the United States. Those with the lowest probability of migrating internationally had the most relatives living in Tunkás. Thus, family ties pull Tunkaseños in both directions. For some potential migrants, such ties anchor them more firmly in the home community; for others they provide an incentive to migrate to the United States in order to reunify with family members already living there. U.S. labor market conditions were related to migration propensity but their influence was not statistically significant.

Finally, we found that substantial numbers of Tunkasenos were opting for internal migration (to nearby tourist cities like Cancún) rather than venturing off to a foreign country. The increased use of internal migration as a substitute for international migration is one of the factors reducing the pool of potential U.S.-bound migrants in Tunkás, together with the fact that Tunkasenos with the highest propensity to migrate to the United States have already gone north during the last two decades, with most opting to stay there indefinitely. Those still going to the United States without legal authorization are still getting in. As in all previous MMFRP studies since 2005, we found that nine out of ten undocumented migrants from Tunkás were able to enter the United States, most on their first try, on their most recent trip to the border (see National Research Council, 2011: 33).

In Chapter 2 we present the results of the MMFRP's most exhaustive study of the factors influencing educational attainment on both sides of the border, with special attention to parental involvement, school and teacher quality, and the influence of having an absent, U.S.-migrant parent.[4] We found that young Tunkaseños are completing more years of schooling than ever before, but significant obstacles to educational advancement remain in place, including poor school facilities, the costs that families must cover to keep their children in school, teen pregnancy, and adolescent drug and alcohol use. Since our initial field study in Tunkás, substance use has become a worrisome problem for both teachers and parents. Two of the key risk factors are relatively easy access to drugs and alcohol for adolescents in Tunkás, and inadequate parental supervision -- especially in families where at least one parent is absent due to migration. We found that having a migrant parent made it more likely that Tunkaseño youths will consume alcohol and drugs, negatively impacting their academic performance.

Chapter 3 explores the U.S. side of the equation, by focusing on the risk factors for drug and alcohol use among California-based migrants, regardless of age, who originated in Tunkás. Drawing on extensive qualitative interviews, the authors emphasize the pressures generated by the U.S. work place, wage labor, and the new social networks formed by migrants in the United States. They find that structural factors like the lack of legal status in the United States (Tunkaseño migrants are predominantly undocumented) cause higher levels of stress and increase vulnerability to substance use. They document the use of alcohol and drugs by migrants as a daily routine for coping with work-related tensions and creating a state of relaxation that can

---

[4] Previous MMFRP research on migration and educational attainment is reported in Sawyer, et al. (2009), Silva, et al. (2010), and Kosnac, et al. (2015: 99-126).

keep them productive during the next work day. They find that the consistent income made possible by a wage-earning job – an income considerably higher than what they had in Tunkás – is an essential factor facilitating migrants' access to alcohol and drugs in the United States. Workplace-based peer pressure motivates many migrants to spend a significant proportion of their income on drugs, despite their desire to save as much money as possible. Finally, the authors explore the influence of returned migrants from the United States on spending and consumption patterns in Tunkás. The returnee brings prestige as well as economic resources to access drugs and alcohol, and may induce other members of his home community to adopt his drug and alcohol use practices.

The final chapter of this book explores an entirely new area for MMFRP research: how global climate change is affecting Tunkaseños' livelihoods and their propensity to migrate internationally. Most economically active residents of Tunkás are employed in agriculture and/or apiculture (bee-keeping and honey production). Using both survey and qualitative interview data, the authors show that more intense heat, hard (and premature) frosts, decreasing precipitation, and other threats to the town's ecosystem associated with climate change are decreasing the profitability of agriculture and apiculture, even as Tunkaseños devote more time to production and spend more money on inputs needed to generate income from these activities. The recent increase in local climate variability is decimating the flora that beekeepers depend upon for honey production, while encouraging voracious pests to destroy whatever farmers can produce from their fields. The authors also illuminate the link between climate change and migration behavior. They find that greater perceived difficulty in extracting value from the land is associated with a higher probability of migrating to the United States. They conclude that the combination of disdain for agricultural labor among the youngest generation of Tunkaseños and greater climate variability could render obsolete the agricultural livelihood upon which the town's residents have depended for centuries.

ACKNOWLEDGMENTS

This study was made possible by a generous grant from Avina Américas and its CAMMINA program (Alianza para las Migraciones en Centroamérica y México), a coalition of social investors and philanthropic organizations. Additional support was provided by the Office of the President, University of California, via the Center for Comparative Immigration Studies (CCIS) at the University of California-San Diego. CCIS has been the MMFRP's institutional home since the program was established in 2004, and the Center's Management Services Officer, Ana Minvielle, provided essential administrative support for our 2014-15 project. We appreciate the continuing support of CCIS Co-Directors John Skrentny and David FitzGerald for the MMFRP. We are also grateful to Dr. Carol Padden, UC San Diego's Dean of Social Sciences, for providing supplemental financial support in her previous role as interim Vice Chancellor for Diversity, Equality, and Inclusion.

This study would not have been possible without the assistance provided in the state of Yucatán by Dr. Pedro Lewin-Fischer, Profesor-Investigador in the Instituto Nacional de Antropología e Historia, Centro INAH Yucatán, and his students. Professor Lewin-Fischer has been the MMFRP's principal Mexico-based collaborator for all four of our field studies in the town of Tunkás. He served as our liaison with municipal officials in Tunkás, three of whom were especially helpful to our 2015 project: María Elena Domínguez Kuh, Presidenta Municipal; Eduardo Cupul, Secretario Municipal; and Raymundo Leal Mena, Síndico Municipal. Professor Lewin-Fischer's steadfast good cheer, expertise, and commitment to the MMFRP over the decade of our fieldwork in Yucatán are deeply appreciated.

Another important contributor to the MMFRP's 2014-15 project -- and previous field studies in Tunkás -- was Professor María Luisa Zúñiga, Campus Director of the Joint Doctoral Program in Interdisciplinary Research on Substance Use, based in the School of Social Work at San Diego State University. Dr. Zúñiga was instrumental in creating our working group on risk behaviors and mental health among adolescent youths in migrating families. She also co-authored this volume's chapter on that subject.

Professor Debra Cornelius, sociologist at Shippensburg State University, was an active participant in the MMFRP's 2012, 2013, and 2015 field studies, providing invaluable assistance with field interviewer supervision. She helped to advise MMFRP students studying occupational health, women's health, and other topics, staying in close touch with them after their graduation from the program. She also provided helpful comments on draft questionnaires and book chapters based on our field research. My husband Jer has been a stalwart supporter of this project at every stage. He participated enthusiastically in the Tunkás fieldwork, adding much-needed levity, and his common-sense advice was gratefully accepted (mostly).

Micah Gell-Redman, Hillary Kosnac, and Veronica Noriega all had key leadership roles throughout the MMFRP's 2014-15 project. Dr. Gell-Redman ably led the instructional component of the program. Ms. Kosnac played an essential role in all phases of the project, from questionnaire construction to mapping and documenting all household units in Tunkás, inputting and analyzing the data, leading our working group on education, and organizing MMFRP students for community outreach. Her organizational skill, energy, and attention to detail were indispensable to the project's success. Ms. Noriega led our working group on U.S. immigration policy and its impacts on migration behavior and also provided essential assistance with fieldwork supervision, data analysis, and logistics. Sandy García, our

Undergraduate Intern for 2014-15, led our working group on substance abuse and contributed to the project in many other ways. As I end my career as a student of Mexican migration to the United States, four decades after it began in nine dusty villages in the Los Altos de Jalisco region, I look back on the more than the nearly 500 students who have accompanied me on that journey. Graduate students, but mostly undergraduates, recruited from Harvard, MIT, Princeton, UC San Diego, UCLA, UC Berkeley, San Diego State University, and a half-dozen Mexican partner institutions, they were the essential actors in the two dozen field studies that I have directed in Mexico. The books and articles based on the field data that these students worked so hard to collect, publications which they largely authored, have brought the world of Mexican migrants and the transnational communities to which they belong to the attention of a multitude of scholars, teachers, public decision-makers, health practitioners, journalists, community organizers, immigration lawyers, members of faith-based communities, and many others. To these students I owe my deep gratitude and my best wishes in pursuing careers that will make a difference in the lives of countless migrants and their children, on both sides of the border.

Of course, our most fundamental debt is owed to the many thousands of people in our Mexican research sites and their satellite communities in the United States who gave generously of their time to be interviewed in our field studies. We worked hard to gain their trust, and they reciprocated with an extraordinary willingness to share life experiences that were often painful to recall. Our *entrevistados* never failed to impress and inspire us with their courage, sacrifice, and tenacity. We hope that we have been faithful stewards and communicators of the knowledge that they entrusted to us. Their stories richly deserved to be told.

Portland, Oregon
October 2, 2015

REFERENCES CITED

Castillo, G., Jiménez-Pacheco, Z., & Pasillas, P. (2007). Stay-at-homes: Why many people do not migrate. Pp. 141-49 in W. Cornelius, D. Fitzgerald, & P. Lewin-Fischer, eds., *Mayan Journeys: The New Migration from Yucatán to the United States*. La Jolla, CA and Boulder, CO: Center for Comparative Immigration Studies,. University of California-San Diego, and Lynne Rienner Publishers.

Kosnac, H., Cornelius, W., Wong, T., Gell-Redman, M., & Hughes, D. (2015). *One Step In and One Step Out: The Lived Experience of Immigrant Participants in the Deferred Action for Childhood Arrivals (DACA) Program*. La Jolla, CA: Center for Comparative Immigration Studies, University of California-San Diego.

Krogstad, J., & Passel, J. (2014). U.S. border apprehensions of Mexicans fall to historic lows. *Fact Sheet*, Pew Research Center, Washington, DC, December 30. http://www.pewresearch.org/fact-tank/2014/12/30/u-s-border-apprehensions-of-mexicans-fall-to-historic-lows/

Li-Ng, J., & Salgado-Torres, A. (2015). Remesas alcanzan máximo crecimiento y registro del año. *Flash Migración México*, BBVA Research, Fundación BBVA Bancomer, October 1.

National Research Council (2011). *Budgeting for Immigration Enforcement: A Path to Better Performance.* Washington, DC: National Academies Press.

Sawyer, A., Keyes, D., Velázquez, C., Lima, G., & Bautista, M. (2009). Going to school, going to *El Norte*: Migration's impact on Tlacotepense education. Pp. 123-64 in *Migration from the Mexican Mixteca: A Transnational Community in Oaxaca and California*, eds. W. Cornelius, D. Fitzgerald, J. Hernández-Díaz, & S. Borger. Jolla, CA and Boulder, CO: Center for Comparative Immigration Studies,. University of California-San Diego, and Lynne Rienner Publishers.

Silva, T., Chang, C., Osuna, C., & Solís-Sosa, I. (2010) Leaving to learn or learning to leave: Education in Tunkás. Pp. 131-58 in *Mexican Migration and the U.S. Economic Crisis: A Transnational Perspective*, eds. W. Cornelius, D. FitzGerald, P. Lewin-Fischer, & L. Muse-Orlinoff. La Jolla, CA, and Boulder, CO: Center for Comparative Immigration Studies, University of California-San Diego, and Lynne Rienner Publishers.

Tunkaseña crosses the town's soccer field.

(Photo by Debra A. Cornelius)

1

U.S. Immigration Policy and the New Calculus of Staying Home in Mexico

VERÓNICA NORIEGA, NAJELY GÓMEZ, ALYSSA KROEGER, CARLOS LEÓN, ANGIE UREÑA, AND ALEX VIVONA

While the vast majority of research on Mexico-to-U.S. migration behavior has focused on the decision to migrate, in this chapter we consider the decision to forego migration, either temporarily or indefinitely. Our interest is in the people who have chosen *not* to migrate to the United States, especially without authorization. We argue that potential migrants are being influenced by a new calculus of staying home in Mexico, resulting from a confluence of macroeconomic factors, U.S. immigration control policies, and family dynamics that constrain mobility.

Our research differs from previous studies of Mexico's "stay-at-homes," which have focused on individual-level, socio-economic and cultural attributes that tend to root people in their home community, such as advanced age, poor health, lack of resources to finance migration, inadequate access to transnational social networks that support migration, lack of English competence, family obligations, and cultural practices. Going beyond these "traditional" determinants of the decision not to migrate, we examine the effects of policy variables (changes in U.S. immigration control policies and enforcement practices), macroeconomic forces (changing U.S. and Mexican labor market conditions), perceptions of physical risk (border violence, criminal activities by people-smugglers, natural hazards) associated with clandestine border crossings, more favorable perceptions of migration to destinations within Mexico as an alternative to migration to the United States, and social networks as an anchoring factor rather than something that drives migration. We hypothesize that the addition of these non-traditional factors to traditional discouragement factors has created a new calculus of staying home in Mexico in the post-2009 period.

RECENT TRENDS IN MEXICO-TO-U.S. MIGRATION

Beginning in 2007 there was a sharp decline in new migration from Mexico. Departures for the United States dropped to levels not seen since the early 1970s. From 2006 to 2008 migration decreased by almost 40 percent. Until this point, Mexican migration had risen steadily since the 1970's, a trend that intensified in the 1990s. Some analyses suggested that migrants were returning to Mexico in large numbers. For example, the Pew Hispanic Center estimated that, from 2005 to 2010, net migration between Mexico and the United States dropped to zero (Passel, D'Vera, & González-Barrera, 2012). The reduced flow of new migrants was reflected in a decline of approximately 1 million in the stock of unauthorized Mexicans living in the United States, from a peak of 6.9 million in 2007 to 5.9 million in 2012 (González-Barrera, A., & Krogstad, J. 2015). This decline mirrored what was happening in the overall population of undocumented immigrants living in the United States, which shrank from a peak of 12.1 million in 2007 to 11.3 in 2014. By 2015, China and India had overtaken Mexico as the top sources of documented immigration to the United States (Chishti & Hipsman, 2015).

Numerous journalists and research analysts quickly blamed the Great Recession in the United States that erupted in December 2007 for this sharp contraction in the migration flow from Mexico. Technically, the Great Recession began in December 2007 and ended in June 2009 -- a 19-month period.[5] However, the end of the recession has not brought a strong rebound in Mexico-to-U.S. migration flows. According to estimates by the Migration Policy Institute, between 2008 and 2009, 6.4 migrants per 1,000 residents of Mexico departed that country. The emigration rate declined to 3.4 per thousand between 2011 and 2012 and remained at 3.3 migrants per 1,000 Mexicans from 2012 to 2014 (Papademetriou & Terrazas 2009).

---

[5] The drop in Mexican migration probably started before the Great Recession technically began, since certain sectors of the U.S. economy in which many Mexican immigrants have been heavily employed, like construction, began shedding jobs before the rest of the U.S. economy.

In Tunkás, migration to the United States originated with the "Bracero Program" of contract importation by the United States, which operated in various forms between 1942 and 1964. According to Silva, Niño and Solís (2007), the number of *braceros* originating in Tunkás was small, but this early flow created a precedent for future migration to the southern California cities of Anaheim and Inglewood, where Tunkaseño braceros first found employment.

The number of migrants leaving Tunkás for the United States remained relatively constant during the 1970s and 1980s, but migration increased significantly in the late 1990s. Tunkaseños, like other Mexicans migrants, were attracted by the abundance of low-skilled jobs created by the U.S. economic boom of the second half of that decade, which was also a period when the financial cost and physical risks of clandestine entry were relatively low. Furthermore, the saturation of the domestic labor market, especially in the tourist cities of the Mayan Rivera and Mérida, encouraged migration to the United States (Muse-Orlinoff & Lewin-Fischer, 2010).

These trends are reflected in data from the migration histories provided by our Tunkaseño interviewees. As shown in Figure 1.1, Tunkaseño migration to the United States rose steadily until 2006, after which the number of trips dropped sharply. Except for one year, departures for the United States have not recovered to pre-Great Recession levels.

Figure 1.1: Tunkaseños' Trips to the United States for Work or Residence, by Year of Departure

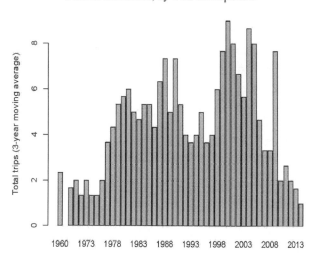

3

Moreover, the proportion of Tunkás residents who expressed an intention to migrate to the United States during the 12 months following their interview dropped from 16.8 percent in the MMFRP's 2006 survey of the town to 7.4 percent in 2009, 4.6 percent in 2012, and just 2.5 percent in our most recent (2015) survey. The steepest decline in intention to migrate occurred between 2006 and 2009, precisely when the Great Recession was taking hold in the United States.

Figure 1.2: Tunkaseños Who Intend to Migrate to the U.S. in Next 12 Months, by Year of Survey (percentages)

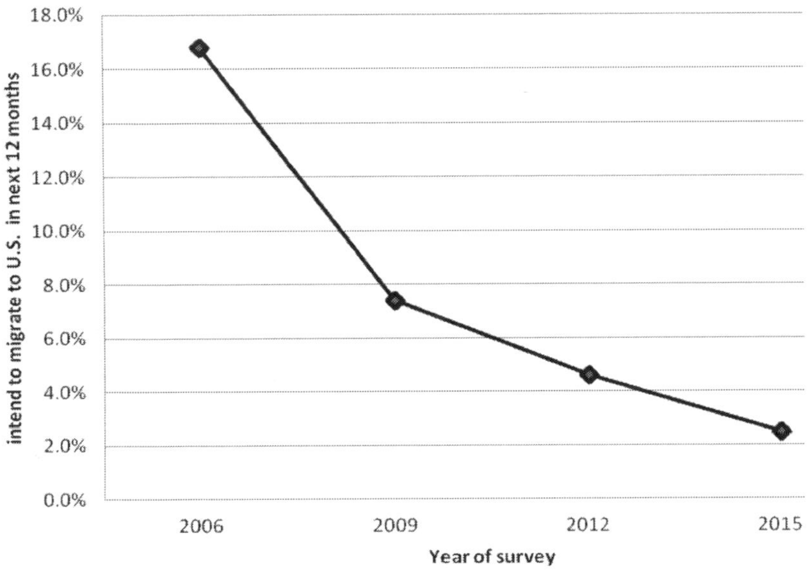

While U.S.-bound migration from Tunkás and other rural Mexican communities declined in tandem with the intensification of the Great Recession, that economic shock may not have been solely responsible. Other factors might have been at work, which could also help explain why Mexico-to-U.S. migration has failed to rebound as strongly as expected once the Great Recession ended.[6] We posit that there is no adequate, single-factor explanation for the sea change in Mexico-to-U.S. migration flows observed since 2007; more likely, complex causation is at work.

---

[6] Such expectations were grounded in history. After all previous economic contractions in the United States in recent decades there was a relatively quick rebound in undocumented migration from Mexico (see Papademetriou & Terrazas 2009).

4

EXPLAINING REDUCED MIGRATION TO THE UNITED STATES: SEVEN DISCOURAGEMENT FACTORS

Drawing on our fieldwork in Tunkás and its satellite communities in southern California, as well as published literature, we have identified seven factors that may enter into the new calculus of staying home in Mexico.

1) Weakness in the low-skilled U.S. job market. Numerous scholars have argued that migration to the U.S. is driven by Mexico/U.S. differentials in labor demand and wages. In the case of Mexican undocumented migration, Hanson (2009) and Preston (2009) have observed that people without documents migrate during economic boom periods and decide to stay home during periods of economic crisis. Because supply is increasing, employers find it easier to hire low-skilled, undocumented workers during periods of robust economic growth. Furthermore, the neoclassical theory of migration argues that countries with an over-supply of workers are prone to send migrants to countries with tight labor supplies (Massey, et al., 1993). Martin and Abella (2006) found that while job and wage-related factors are most significant at the beginning of an international migration flow, over time transborder social networks and family ties start to play a major role, making the migration flow less sensitive to labor market fluctuations.

In the case of Mexican migration, the low-skilled labor market in the United States has recovered very slowly in the aftermath of the Great Recession. By 2014, sectors of the U.S. economy that traditionally employed an important share of the Latino population (such as the construction industry) had started to recover, but few of the jobs being added were filled by immigrants (Kochhar, 2014). While the unemployment rate among foreign-born Latinos has declined, it has not returned to pre-Great Recession levels. Unemployment among immigrant Latinos rose from 6.8 percent in the fourth quarter of 2007 to 13.8 percent in the fourth quarter of 2009, declining to 10.3 percent by the fourth quarter of 2013. It is therefore plausible that potential migrants have decided to stay put in Mexico due to the relative weakness of U.S. labor demand, especially in sectors of the economy where Latino immigrants have traditionally been employed.

2) Changes in intensity and types of U.S. immigration enforcement. The sharp rise in unauthorized immigration that the United States experienced until the last decade of the 20th Century fueled an increase in U.S. immigration enforcement efforts, both at the U.S.-Mexico border and in the country's interior. This trend accelerated after the terrorist attacks of 9/11, which made the porosity of the southwestern border a potent political issue. Not only were more Border Patrol agents, hardware, and new surveillance technologies added to the enforcement effort; in recent years there has also been a sustained effort to heighten the penalties for illegal entry and re-entry. The Border Patrol has implemented a "Consequence Delivery System," in which far more migrants are being prosecuted rather than given the opportunity for "voluntary departure", thereby criminalizing migrant entry and reentry. During the presidency of Barack Obama, deportations have averaged about 400,000 per year, with more apprehensions being made away from the border area, in residential areas and workplaces. For example, the proportion of unauthorized Mexicans apprehended most recently at work or at home rose from 3 percent in 2005 to 17 percent in 2010 (see Passel et al., 2012, Figure 3.2). Moreover, to reduce recidivism, U.S. authorities lengthened bans on (legal) re-entry for deported immigrants to ten years or more.

While the number of Border Patrol agents and other enforcement resources deployed along the U.S.-Mexico border have continued to grow (there were 20,863 Border Patrol agents in Fiscal Year 2014), the number of migrant apprehensions fell from 1,189,075 in FY 2005 to 340,252 in FY 2011.[7] Government officials claimed that the sharp drop in apprehensions was due mainly to enhanced enforcement efforts. It is possible that the gradual build-up of U.S. immigration enforcement efforts since 1993 has reached a "deterrence tipping point," beyond which potential migrants are discouraged from attempting to cross into the United States by the increased likelihood of apprehension and the tougher penalties being imposed on those who are caught. However, direct evidence is lacking to support this claim. Apprehension statistics do not include migrants who succeed in entering without detection, which according to previous MMFRP studies account for more than nine out of ten unauthorized migrants who come to the border seeking entry into the United States (see National Research Council 2011: 33; Hicken, Cohen, & Narvaez, 2010). Moreover, "the stated aim of reducing the flow and stock of un-authorized immigrants through a robust deterrence strategy has not been achieved" (Cornelius & Salehyan, 2007). Nevertheless, it is possible that the consequences of strong border enforcement, such as raising the cost and risks of clandestine entry, play a role in the new calculus of staying home in Mexico.

---

[7] Apprehensions rebounded modestly, to 486,651, in FY 2014.

3) Remote Deterrence. Heightening the physical risks associated with unauthorized border crossings, by forcing them to be made in areas where life-threatening natural hazards like extreme heat and cold are likely to be encountered, has been part of the U.S. strategy to discourage potential migrants since the mid-1990s (Cornelius, 2001). Officially called "prevention through deterrence," the strategy has been characterized by academic researchers as "remote deterrence," defined as efforts intended to dissuade potential migrants from ever deciding to leave their homes in the first place (Hicken et al., 2011; Fischbein, et al., 2013: 27). The tightening of U.S. border security near urban ports of entry has shifted undocumented migration toward remote regions such as the Sonoran Desert of Arizona, California's Imperial Valley Desert, and the Tecate Mountains east of San Diego, where security is weaker but crossing conditions are more difficult.[8] However, Cornelius and Salehyan (2007) found that "perceptions of the danger and difficultly involved in clandestine crossings have not discouraged migrants from attempting them." Indeed, all previous MMFRP studies have found that perceptions of border-crossing danger and difficulty are not statistically significant influences on migration behavior, being far outweighed by economic and family-related incentives to migrate.

Another factor contributing to physical risks for potential migrants is the rise in violence on the Mexican side of the border, ever since Mexican President Felipe Calderón declared a "war against organized crime," especially the drug cartels. From 2006 to 2010 the six Mexican states located at the U.S.-Mexico border accounted for 47.8 percent of all drug-related murders in Mexico, despite having only 17.6 percent of the country's population (Rios Contreras, 2014: 201). About 60,000 drug-war-related deaths were recorded, mostly in northern Mexico, between December 2006 and December 2012 (Fitzgerald & Alarcón 2013: 122). Moreover, Mexican criminal organizations have diversified their activities, with kidnapping and extortion becoming highly lucrative "side" businesses. U.S.-based relatives of kidnapped migrants are called upon to pay ransoms. Moreover, migrants headed to the United States have long been preyed upon by

---

[8] Between 1998 and 2014, more than 6,000 migrants have died in the deserts or mountains of the U.S. Southwest, attempting to cross into the United States from Mexico (Sacchetti, 2014). However, fatalities at the border dropped to an all-time low in 2014, with 307 deaths compared to 445 in 2013 (Galván, 2014). The reduced death toll almost certainly reflects fewer entry attempts being made.

bandits operating in the borderlands who are not part of organized crime organizations. In a previous MMFRP study survey respondents cited running into Mexican bandits as one of their top concerns when contemplating an unauthorized border crossing (Kosnac, Mejorado, Davidson, Marroquín & Nazario, 2013), Thus, potential migrants may be discouraged by the higher risks to their personal safety -- as well as to their relatives' financial well being -- resulting from organized crime and banditry in the borderlands.

4) Changes in the people-smuggling industry that increase the cost and risks of illegal border crossings. As noted above, drug cartels have been venturing into new businesses, including people-smuggling. Before the early 1990s, the people-smuggling industry was dominated by relatively small operations anchored in migrant-sending communities (Fuentes & Garcia, 2009: 80). Prospective migrants found their coyotes mainly through referrals from relatives or friends, often in the same communities where they lived. However, since the implementation of the "prevention through deterrence" immigration control strategy beginning in 1993, larger-scale, professional people-smuggling businesses – some related to drug cartels, some not -- have gained market share.

U.S officials have frequently blamed migrant border-crossing fatalities on the irresponsibility and cruelty of smugglers connected to organized criminal organizations, contrasted with the family-vetted, "mom and pop" people-smugglers who traditionally dominated the industry (López Castro, 1998). What is indisputable is that people-smugglers can charge far more today for their services than in earlier eras of Mexico-to-U.S. migration. Between 1995 and 2004 the average price of hiring a smuggler rose from $490 to between $2,000 and $2,500 (Cornelius, 2004:13). Higher profit margins have inspired criminal organizations to become involved in human smuggling (Andreas, 2001). These commercial smuggling organizations may also be involved in drug smuggling, but human and drug smuggling operations often do not overlap (Fuentes & Garcia, 2009: 98).[9]

---

[9] Fieldwork conducted in the late 1990s for a binational study of Mexico-to-U.S. migration found "no evidence of collaboration between coyotes and drug traffickers in the towns [from which migrants come]," with local coyotes embedded in migrant-sending communities "keeping their distance…because of the high risks involved in drug smuggling (López Castro 1998: 972).

The extent to which the involvement of criminal organizations in the human smuggling industry has led to higher migrant injuries and deaths is contested. Many, perhaps a majority, of undocumented migrants see people-smugglers not as predators but as necessary service-providers and risk-reducers (Fuentes & García, 2009; Kaye, 201). David Spener (2009: 197) argues, based on extensive ethnographic research, that large and organized smuggling operations generally do not present a heightened security risk for migrants. However, once their clients arrive in the United States, smugglers may have the opportunity to exploit migrants' fear of being detected by immigration authorities by charging a higher fee (Spener, 2009: 189).

If the people-smuggling industry has evolved into larger-scale operations, at least some of which are also involved in drug smuggling, it is possible that prospective migrants would have relatively less access to a "safe" and reliable smuggler who has been procured for them by family or friends. Moreover, criminal organizations' involvement in people-smuggling may expose the migrant to kidnapping, extortion, robbery, or rape – all which could be potential discouragement factors when deciding whether to migrate.

5) Improved labor market and living conditions in Mexico. Some scholars, journalists, and research organizations have argued that the recent decline in Mexico-to-U.S. migration can be attributed to the fact that the Mexican economy has been growing at a respectable pace – indeed, recovering faster than the United States from the Great Recession – with low inflation. According to the World Bank, Mexico's GDP grew by 5.1 percent in 2010 and 4.0 percent in 2011 and 2012. However, it experienced very little growth in 2013 (1.1 percent) and 2014 (2.1 percent). Mexican President Felipe Calderón claimed in 2012 that net Mexico-to-U.S. migration had dropped to zero, in part due to the fact that his administration had created more employment opportunities[10] and expanded the educational system, thus providing the Mexican population with viable alternatives to migrating to the United States (Olson, 2012; Chishti & Hipsman, 2015). Furthermore, as Eyzaguirre (2011) points out, standards of living in Mexico and other Latin American countries have been rising as a consequence of expanded government cash transfers to the poor.

---

[10] Other observers noted that most of these new jobs were being created in places and occupations that would be unlikely to provide employment for significant numbers of potential U.S.-bound migrants, especially residents of small, rural communities.

Thus, it is possible that the economic push factors that drove four generations of Mexicans to migrate to the United States may have diminished in intensity, due to the relatively strong performance of the Mexican economy in recent years, coupled with greater government assistance to the poorest Mexicans. Growth in formal-sector manufacturing and service jobs not only offers potential migrants the possibility of earning higher wages; it also eliminates the extra costs, risks, and potentially hostile receptions involved in seeking work in the United States and makes it possible to stay closer to their families. Nevertheless, it is important to note that the Mexican public's *perception* of the domestic labor market has remained pessimistic.[11] And despite stepped-up government spending on income-transfer programs, persistent poverty and low wages continue to force rural Mexicans to migrate internationally. Staying home simply may not be a realistic option for many of them (Bacon 2013).

6) Internal migration as a substitute for international migration. If the Mexican economy is doing better and barriers to entry into the United States are higher, it is possible that rural dwellers might prefer to migrate to cities within Mexico to search for employment. According to the United Nations Development Program, internal migration involves six times more Mexicans than international migration, with 500,000 people migrating internally per year (Rivero-Fuentes, 2005). However, there is a paucity of research that directly addresses the decision to migrate internally vs. internationally.

Migrating to domestic destinations removes some stressors for would-be international migrants, such as being separated from family members for long periods and having to work in a place with a different language and strange customs. Additionally, by staying in Mexico, would-be international migrants can avoid the psychological stress of living in the shadows, constantly fearful of apprehension and deportation. But internal migration has it disadvantages. For example, there is a lack of variety in employment opportunities. The most commonly available occupations are chef, carpenter, and construction worker – jobs in which migrants are paid less than if they worked in the same occupation in the United States. Furthermore, a previous study of Tunkaseños found that many who have migrated internally feel that they have little

---

[11] Consulta Mitofsky, a widely respected Mexican survey research organization, found that in 2011, 82 percent of Mexicans said the economic situation in their country was getting worse, up from 60 percent who said the same in 2006 and 57 percent who said so in 2001 (Passel et al., 2012: 34).

control over their own schedule and work methods, compared to when they worked in agriculture in Tunkás (Rodríguez et al., 2007).

A person's socioeconomic status can determine whether he/she migrates within Mexico or to the United States. Those lacking enough money to migrate to the United States – mostly to pay a people-smuggler for border-crossing assistance – are more likely to end up working in Mexican cities. Nevertheless, migration to destinations within Mexico can act as a springboard for future international migration. Tunkaseños who migrate internally learn how to manage money well enough to cover all expenses and still send money home. Moreover, Tunkaseños who find work in international tourist destinations such as Cancún and Playa del Carmen are exposed to English-speaking tourists through work in the hospitality and tourist industries. This helps them acquire the English that they will need for future migration to the United States (Rodriguez, Wittlinger, & Manzanero Rodriguez, 2007). In addition, "internal migration allows rural-origin migrants to ease into the migration experience, rather than have to confront the risks and shocks associated with international migration unprepared" (Rodríguez et al., 2007: 79). When migrants are exposed to environments that are similar to those in the United States, they have more knowledge about the circumstances and lifestyles they will confront in the United States. Thus, internal migration may serve as a "school" for cross-border migration.

7) Family ties. The importance of family ties in decisions to migrate and to return to one's place of origin has been emphasized by practitioners of the social capital theory of migration (see, for example, Massey 1998, McKeown, 1999). Kosnac et al. (2013) found that a lack of social network contacts in the United States strongly influences the decision to return to one's place of origin after a period of U.S. employment. Social networks are important because family and friends in the host country can provide direct assistance to migrants in their search for jobs, housing, and services like child care (Davis, Stecklo & Winters 2002; Hanson, 2009). However, in communities like Tunkás that have a shorter history of migration to the United States, the effects of network contacts might be significantly weaker, since it is possible that transnational social networks have not matured and a larger part of the immediate and extended family remains in Mexico. Thus, strong family ties, centered on the community of origin rather than the United States, could potentially discourage international migration. Potential migrants simply may not want to be separated from their immediate

11

family members. Indeed, according to a previous study in Tunkás, "family solidarity and family obligations exert a strong effect to keep potential migrants rooted in [Mexico]" (Castillo, Jiménez-Pacheco & Pasillas, 2007: 141). Thus, we posit that family ties can either encourage or discourage international migration, depending on the locus and density of such connections.

EXPLAINING THE DECISION TO STAY HOME

Our survey found that the majority of Tunkaseño residents had never tried to migrate to the United States to live or work. While Tunkaseños have been migrating to the United States since the 1970s, only one in five (22.4 percent) of those whom we interviewed in 2015 had any history of international migration. (Of course, those who have emigrated permanently to the U.S. were not present to be interviewed.) Among those who had migrated to the United States at least once, the median year of their first trip was 1988, which reflects the relatively short history of Tunkás as a community of international migration. By contrast, the median year of Tunkaseño migrants' most recent trip is 1996, suggesting that the most Tunkaseños entered the migratory stream for the first time during the U.S. economic boom of the mid-to-late 1990s. Two southern California cities, Anaheim (Orange County) and Inglewood (a small city that is part of the Los Angeles metropolitan area) and places close to them continue to be preferred destinations for Tunkaseños: 27.4 percent of our interviewees went to Inglewood while 25.6 percent chose Anaheim. The city of Los Angeles was the third most common destination, accounting for 12.8 percent.

Their motivations for going north are similar to those of the vast majority of Mexican migrants to the United States over many generations. Most of our migrant interviewees reported that the main reason for their most recent trip to the United States was to search for better employment opportunities (27.4 percent), to earn higher wages (23.4 percent), or to reunite with family members already living in the United States (20.5 percent). Also, like the majority of Mexican migrants, Tunkaseños tend to migrate to the United States without legal documents. Around three-quarters of our respondents (77 percent) reported not having legal documents to enter the United States on their most recent trip.

Tunkaseños who choose *not* to go to the United States seem less motivated by economic concerns and more sensitive to their social networks. As shown in Figure 1.3, the most frequently mentioned reason for staying in Tunkás was a lack of relatives and friends in the United States (27.4 percent), followed by a preference for the quiet, peaceful lifestyle of Tunkás (21.3 percent), and a lack of legal authorization to enter the United States (9.5 percent).

Figure 1.3: Most important reason why Tunkaseños did not want to go to the United States in 2015

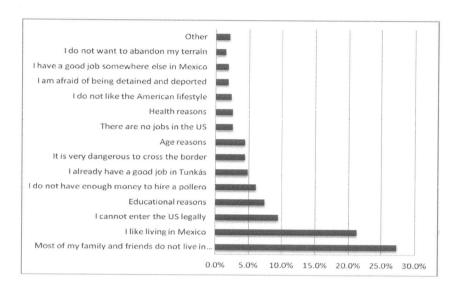

In order to assess how our seven hypothesized factors shape the decision to migrate, we constructed a summative index of "propensity to migrate to the United States"[12] and created two groups for analysis, i.e., those who scored above and below the median value on this index. We created two additional groups to have a more comprehensive picture of migration behavior in Tunkás: "complete non-migrants" (people who have no domestic or international migration experience at all and are of prime migration age, 18-25 years old), and "Internal migrants" (persons having only internal migration experience). In Table 1.1 we report the socio-demographic characteristics of these four subpopulations. Significance levels for inter-group

---

[12] The index aggregates the respondent's prior migration history (e.g., having ever migrated to the United States, the number of trips in the last five years), the total amount of time the respondent has spent in the United States (normalized to preserve scale), whether the respondent intends to migrate in the next 12 months, and whether or not the respondent is of prime migration age, which we define as being 18-35 years old.

differences, by t-test, are also reported. In the following sections we discuss these inter-group differences with reference to the seven Mexico-to-U.S. migration discouragement factors posited above.

Table 1.1: Socio-demographic Characteristics of Tunkaseños by Migration Behavior

	Low propensity to migrate to U.S.	High propensity to migrate to U.S.	Complete non-migrants	Internal migrants
Undocumented currently	100.0%***	95.2%***	100.0% *	-----
Undocumented on first trip to U.S.	-----	85.7%	-----	-----
Age (mean)	43.8 ***	36 ***	26.8	37.6 **
Gender: male	32.1%***	52.8% ***	29.8%	44.0%
Married	63.2%	64.3%	63.6%	55.6%*
Have children: yes	75.5%	71.3%	65.7%	66.7% *
Relatives in Mexico (mean)	8.7 **	7.8 **	9**	8.3
Relatives in the U.S. (mean)	0.6 ***	1.4 ***	0.2 **	0.4***
Highest education level (years)	8.0 ***	10.1 ***	10.1***	10.4***
Wealth (mean # of household items possessed)[13]	5.0	4.4	5.2	5.5***

*p< .05; **p <.01; ***p<.001

---

[13] Household items include transportation vehicles, TVs, DVDs, personal computers, Internet access, refrigerator, stove, microwave, washing machine, clothes dryer, hot-water heater, and water tank.

14

Weakness in the Low-skilled U.S. Job Market as a Reason for Staying Home

Given the apparently strong correlation between the Great Recession and the drop in new migration of Tunkaseños to the United States, perceived and experienced changes in the low-skilled U.S. labor market are of particular interest in explaining decisions to remain in Tunkás. A clear majority of our interviewees (55.9 percent) reported that it had not been difficult at all to find their most recent job in the United States. Only one in five (22.5 percent) said they had found it somewhat difficult. Returned migrant Daniel, a 25-year-old Tunkaseño who lived for six years in El Monte, California, recounted how easy it was for him to find a job when he first arrived in the United States in 2007. But he saw how job opportunities collapsed in 2008: "The first year that I was in the U.S. there was a lot of work, but later it started to get slow. The economy was not good due to the crisis."

Comparing low- and high-propensity migrants to the U.S., a higher percentage of those most likely to migrate to the United States agreed with the statement that it is harder to get a job in the United States now than it was five years ago (41.9 percent), compared with 34.6 percent among low-propensity migrants. Complete non-migrants had the most optimistic view of the U.S. job market, perhaps reflecting their lack of direct information on labor market conditions. Not surprisingly, people who are more likely to migrate internationally are better informed about the state of the U.S. economy and its financial struggles since 2008, and tend to be less optimistic when evaluating the U.S. labor market.

As discussed above, social networks play a crucial role in the decision to migrate, since it is through family and friends that migrants are able to acquire housing and job recommendations when they are newly arrived. Most of the Tunkaseños whom we interviewed who had ever lived in the United States reported finding their most recent U.S. job through family and friends (66.4 percent). Moreover, social networks disseminate important information to would-be migrants. We asked Tunkaseños interviewed in Mexico if they knew of any friends or family members living in the United States whose work hours had been reduced due to the Great Recession. Among those with a low propensity to migrate internationally, 42 percent had relatives or friends who had been laid off or experienced cuts in their working hours, compared to 34.4 percent in the high-propensity group. Internal migrants had the highest frequency of family and friends that had suffered the adverse effects of the U.S. economic crisis (46.8 percent). Only 8.9 percent of our interviewees reported that someone in their own household had *returned* from the United States due to a scarcity of work opportunities.

These findings suggest that a weakness in the U.S. labor market (defined as lack of employment opportunities or diminished work hours) might not have been the key motivation for potential Tunkaseño migrants to forego international migration in recent years. Our findings are consistent with previous MMFRP studies in Tunkás. According to Muse-Orlinoff & Lewin-Fischer (2010), Tunkaseños did not experience high levels of layoffs during 2008 and 2009, due to the fact that most of them had found work in the service sector (e.g., car washes), which was not affected as strongly by the Great Recession as other sectors where Mexican migrants typically work, such as the construction industry. Among Tunkaseños interviewed in 2015 who had returned from working in the United States, only 5 percent had been employed in construction, while nearly two-thirds (65.7 percent) had worked in the service sector.[14] Among Tunkaseños whom we interviewed in California, the top-three occupations were in the non-professional services sector (e.g. janitor), followed by restaurant-related work, and housewives. The unemployment rate among those interviewed in the United States was just 3.2 percent at the time our fieldwork (February-March 2015).

In sum, our research suggests that most Tunkaseños have not been significantly affected by the downturn in the supply of low-skilled jobs in the United States. Neither they nor most of their friends and relatives have experienced layoffs or cuts in their work hours. Thus, it is unlikely that Tunkaseños who have decided to stay home in recent years have done so because of an absolute shortage of income-earning opportunities in the United States. Nevertheless, a large majority (71 percent) of our interviewees on both sides of the border believed that finding a job in the United States today is "somewhat difficult" or "very difficult." This perception may be the most important residue of the Great Recession.

---

[14] Kochhar (2014) notes that in some U.S. service industries (e.g., eating, drinking, lodging) and retail trade, Hispanics actually gained jobs during the Great Recession.

Changes in Intensity and Types of U.S. Immigration Enforcement

Our survey data suggest that tightened immigration control measures have not been effective in deterring migration to the United States. Among our undocumented interviewees, it took, on average, 1.9 attempts to successfully enter the United States on their most recent trip to the border, compared with 1.3 attempts on their first trip. Of the 31 interviewees who reported being caught during their most recent trip to the border, more than nine out of ten (93.6 percent) were able to enter undetected on their second or subsequent attempt. This eventual success rate is quite consistent with the findings of previous studies of Tunkaseño migration to the United States (see, for example, Hicken et al., 2010). Among the small fraction of undocumented Tunkaseños interviewed in 2015 who had been apprehended on their most recent entry attempt, a few had experienced abuse at the hands of Border Patrol agents. For example, Fernando, a 30-year-old returned migrant interviewed in Tunkás, reported that while trying to cross the border a second time, Border Patrol agents injured his back: "They kicked me and hit me."

Our interviews with Tunkaseños currently living in Mexico who have a history of migration to the United States revealed that most had crossed the border on foot, through a desert or mountainous area (47.9 percent). But nearly half had entered through a legal port of entry (POE): 38.7 percent moving through a border-crossing gate on foot or in a vehicle, and 9.2 percent passing through an airport. These data suggest continued growth of "undocumented" migration through urban ports of entry vs. remote areas where most of the post-1993 border enforcement build-up has been located. The increasing frequency of unauthorized entries through POEs has been documented in several previous MMFRP studies (Hicken et al., 2010: 60; Hicken et al., 2011: 28; Cornelius et al, 2013: 64). The popularity of this mode of entry has grown because the probability of detection is significantly lower than for a clandestine entry through remote areas, and because a POE crossing sharply reduces the migrant's physical risk.[15]

With regard to immigration enforcement away from the border, the impact on undocumented Tunkaseños has been minimal. When we asked interviewees currently living in the United States, and those who had previously lived there, if they had been

---

[15] Staffing at POEs has grown much less rapidly than Border Patrol staffing between the POEs. In FY 2015 there were 20,672 Customs and Border Protection agents working at POEs, up from 15,893 in FY 2005.

stopped by police in the United States, more than half (54.7 percent) reported having had such an experience. But among those stopped, only one-third (33.9 percent) had been detained (23.4 percent were actually incarcerated), while 60.9 percent were let off with a fine, 26.6 percent had their car confiscated, and just 6 percent were turned over by the police to immigration authorities for deportation.[16] Bernardo, a 42-year-old former people-smuggler, told us that he had been caught and deported once while living in California. Eight days later he was back inside the United States. He also reported that, on another occasion, immigration agents stopped him while he was driving: "I only got a ticket. I paid it, and that was that."

All in all, the mass round-up and deportation efforts of recent years have failed to sweep a significant number of unauthorized Tunkaseño migrants into the net. While police stops are common, only rarely do they put those stopped on a path to deportation. Nine out of ten (91.6 percent) of our interviewees reported that they had never been deported, under any circumstances, and 97.5 percent had no pending deportation order. Of the ten persons interviewed in our 2015 survey who reported having been deported at least once, only four had been brought into immigration court, and most of them were given the opportunity to return to Mexico after signing a voluntary repatriation waiver (vs. being subjected to criminal prosecution or administrative removal). Four interviewees had received a re-entry ban -- an order prohibiting them from re-entering the United States following deportation. But when asked if they were still thinking of returning to the United States, half of them responded affirmatively.

While the personal experience of Tunkaseños and their family and friends with large-scale deportation efforts in the United States was limited, *knowledge* of these efforts was considerably more widespread. More than half of our interviewees (56.4 percent) said that they knew someone who had been deported, and that this person also had received a ban on re-entry, usually for ten years. Interviewees with a low propensity to migrate were the least likely to know someone who had been deported in the last five years (only 16.3 percent). Taken together, these findings suggest that large-scale deportations occurring in the United States since 2005 have had little effect on the lives

---

[16] A previous MMFRP study, based on survey data collected in 2011 in Escondido, a city in northern San Diego County, found a higher incidence of migrants being turned over to immigration authorities after traffic stops: 23.3 percent (García, 2014: 11). Escondido has a history of very close cooperation between local police and immigration agents.

18

of Tunkaseños and thus are unlikely to have discouraged many would-be migrants from going north.

Awareness of mass deportations (vs. actual experience) has complicated effects on migration behavior among our interviewees. Almost half (46.3%) of those with a low propensity to migrate believed that deportations of Mexicans had increased in the last five years, but an even larger share of our high-propensity-to-migrate group -- 62.1 percent – were aware of increased deportations. These results suggest a *positive* correlation between the perception that deportations have risen and the probability of unauthorized migration, a finding consistent with previous MMFRP studies (for example, Hicken et al., 2009: 86-87). Similarly, less than half (47.7 percent) of low-propensity-to-migrate respondents in our sample believed that it is more difficult to cross the border today than it was five years ago, but a clear majority of the high- propensity group believed this (59.7%). Such counter-intuitive findings may be attributable to the fact that people who have already decided to migrate, or have a higher propensity to migrate, are better informed than the rest of the population about U.S. immigration enforcement policies, at least partly because they have more sources of information (i.e., social network contacts) in the United States.

Remote Deterrence

Our interviewees were asked about the various kinds of hazards that they had encountered while trying to cross the border without authorization. Among Tunkaseños interviewed in Mexico, more than one out of ten (11.2 percent) reported that they had been the victim of a robbery, beating, some other type of physical abuse, blackmail, or kidnapping. The most common perpetrators identified by interviewees were organized criminal gangs, followed by Mexican police, U.S. Border Patrol agents, and people-smugglers. While assaults by people-smugglers are infrequent, they occur and are not new. Bernardo remembered his experience while trying to cross the border in 1987: "The coyotes took all our belongings and beat us with their R15 and AK-47 rifles." He also recounted that during another border crossing attempt, in 2001, he saw how coyotes took some of the women from the group and "put them to work."

We presented to our interviewees six cartoons depicting various types of border-crossing hazards, asking them to pick the three most worrisome to a person thinking about crossing the border without authorization (see Figure 1.4). Among respondents with no migration experience, more than one-third (37.9 percent) chose the image of a kidnapping, followed by a person being robbed (25.4 percent), and an image of people being incarcerated -- presumably as a penalty for illegal entry (22.6 percent). These responses are interesting, considering that just 7.5 percent of our respondents knew someone who had actually been kidnapped while trying to enter the United States clandestinely. People with U.S. migration experience selected almost the same images as those with no U.S. experience, the only notable difference being that experienced migrants selected a natural hazard (extreme heat) as the third most worrisome aspect of illegal entry. "It's very difficult to cross," said Víctor, a 63-year-old returned migrant from the United States who now lives in Tunkás. "My son almost died in the desert. He told me that had it not been for another migrant that helped him he would have died."

Figure 1.4: "What does someone thinking about crossing the border without papers worry about most?"

While our data reveal that only a few Tunkaseños have personally experienced abuse when crossing the border, they are more generally aware of the hazards posed by organized crime operating in the borderlands. Stories about kidnapping spread around not only through family and friends but also, perhaps more importantly, through the mass media. As explained by Jorge, a 25-year-old interviewee in Tunkás: "I've heard it on the news. Some coyotes kidnap you and ask for ransom."

Finally, we asked our interviewees for a general assessment of how dangerous it is to cross the border without authorization. More than nine out of ten (92.9 percent) said that currently it is "very dangerous" to cross the border illegally – virtually the same proportion found in the MMFRP's 2012 survey in Tunkás. However, when asked to compare these conditions with those existing five years ago, just 42.3 percent reported that it had been "very dangerous" to cross the border illegally at that time. Nevertheless, when we compare interviewees with a low and high propensity to migrate, we find that 54.9 percent of high-propensity migrants believed that it is more dangerous to cross now then it was five years ago, while less than half of the low-propensity group (44.2 percent) held this belief.

As with perceptions of mass deportations occurring in the United States, a possible explanation for this pattern of responses is that persons who have a higher propensity to migrate internationally are better informed about border-crossing hazards and as a consequence feel more confident to deal with them – especially with assistance from a competent *pollero* (the term for people-smuggler used most commonly in Yucatán). In any event, the evidence from our study supporting "remote deterrence" as a contributor to decisions to stay home is quite mixed.

Changes in the People-smuggling Industry that Increase the Costs and Risks of Illegal Border Crossings

The fees paid by Tunkaseño migrants to their *polleros* have risen sharply since the early 1990s, as shown in Figure 1.5. The steady increase in fees[17] can be attributed largely to the U.S. border enforcement build-up that began in 1993. The fees that can be charged by people-smugglers are a function of the perceived probability of being apprehended by Border Patrol agents. Professional assistance with clandestine entry reduces this probability.

---

[17] The drop in fees since 2008 is probably due to our small sample size in those years.

Figure 1.5: Median Fee Paid to People-smuggler on Most Recent Trip to U.S.

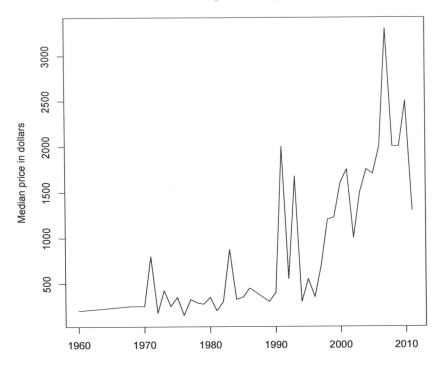

The cost of hiring a *pollero* varies significantly by how the smuggler is found. Among migrants interviewed in our survey, 34.4 percent reported that no one had recommended the pollero that they hired for their most recent trip to the United States (they found them on their own), while 53.4 used a *pollero* recommended by relatives or friends with U.S. migration experience. Although our sample is small, this trend is similar to past MMFRP surveys in Tunkás. For example, in the 2006 survey, 57 percent of migrants found *polleros* with the help of relatives or friends (Kimball et al., 2007: 102). Daniel, one of our 2015 interviewees, recalled his experience:

> "I got the *pollero* through a friend who had previously used [the same *pollero*] to cross. He gave me his number. He asked me where I was and told me how to find him. Altogether there were 20 of us. Everyone was able to cross, walking through the dessert. A car picked us up and we rode for seven hours. I was very tired!

22

Bernardo, himself a former *pollero*, described the process of hiring a smuggler this way:

> You make the trip with someone who knows a *pollero*. You go to Tijuana and contact him there, you tell them how many people there are in your group, and where they are from. Once at the border you give the *pollero* the phone number of a relative in the United States and he contacts the family member. However, they do their research on who is going to pay for the crossing. Not everyone can afford to pay that much [more than $1,000].

We found a large difference between the median price of people-smugglers recommended to migrants by family or friends ($1,400) and those found at the border ($400). This difference is easily explainable. Migrants typically trust people-smugglers recommended to them by relatives or friends more than smugglers found at the border, whose reliability and effectiveness they cannot accurately judge. The sense of trust typically involved in hiring a recommended smuggler is translated into a higher price. Moreover, polleros who are hired on the border without any recommendation have a higher probability of being involved with organized crime (De León, 2012).

Nevertheless, regardless of how they hired them, the vast majority of our interviewees do not seem to have had problems with their *polleros*. When asked if the *pollero* had made good on their agreement, 96.7 percent of our interviewees reported that they did while only 3.3 percent indicated that the *pollero* failed to deliver on his promises, which typically include transportation to the border-crossing site, unlimited attempts to cross (until successful), and, once inside the United States, transportation to a safe house (Fuentes & García, 2009: 91). Moreover, among our interviewees there were no recent reports of people-smugglers physically abusing their clients.

We found no difference in smugglers' performance between those found at the border and those hired through family-and-friends referrals. Even so, the vast majority of our respondents (86 percent) believed that, when compared to the past, more *polleros* today have had contact with organized crime. Both low-propensity-to-migrate and high-propensity interviewees held this belief (84.5 percent and 86.6 percent, respectively). Thus, Roberto, a 37-year-old Tunkaseño, told us: "Nowadays, *polleros* are involved with drug dealers, with all the bad people." Juan, a 20-year-old migrant from Tunkás now living in Cancún, agreed: "*Polleros* are involved with the mafia." Even a former *pollero* living in Tunkás observed: "Everyone is corrupted -- the police, the Border Patrol, and the *polleros*. Everyone works for the same mafia."

This commonly held belief helps to explain why Tunkaseños are willing to pay more to get a *pollero* with good recommendations, rather than hire a cheap one at the border and run the risk of being kidnapped or robbed. But even though smugglers are now perceived to have contact with criminal organizations, their track record of fulfilling their deals with migrant clients is extremely good. Thus, it is hard to conclude from our field data that perceived changes in the people-smuggling industry are significantly influencing the decision to migrate or stay home.

Improved Labor Market and Living Conditions in Mexico as a Reason to Stay Home

Social welfare programs positively influence the growth of the formal sector of the economy, which locates more people in formal institutions of health and education while adding to general labor productivity (Eyzaguirre, 2011; Sen, 1999). Following this argument about the relationship between participation in official anti-poverty programs and improved living standards, we asked our interviewees in Tunkás about their participation in such programs. An overwhelming majority (84.7 percent) reported that there was someone in their household who benefitted from Seguro Popular, Mexico's universal health care program covering all medical costs. More than one-third (36.2 percent) of households reported participating in PROCAMPO, a program that provides direct financial support for small-scale agricultural production, and 45.8 percent indicated that someone in their household participated in Prospera, a program previously called Oportunidades. Prospera is a conditional cash transfer program that gives money to mothers to help support their families and encourages them to maintain regular healthcare for themselves and keep their children enrolled in school. The program recently began assisting students of higher education financially, as well as helping people to find formal employment.

Among our interviewees, complete non-migrants had the highest participation rates in government cash-transfer programs per household (a participation rate of 92.5 percent). Those that have a low propensity to migrate to the United States are more likely (87.3 percent) to participate in government programs than those with a high propensity to migrate internationally (68.0 percent). These findings suggest that people receiving social

24

welfare benefits may prefer to stay home, since they perceive an improvement in their personal and/or their family's economic situation.[18]

While the improvement in social welfare benefits may be cushioning the effects of poverty and inequality in Mexico, these positive effects do not seem to be translating into more positive perceptions of labor market conditions in Mexico. When we asked our interviewees about the current difficulty of finding a job somewhere in the Yucatán peninsula, compared to the conditions of five years ago, most Tunkaseños reported that it is harder to find a job in the Yucatán peninsula now (see Figure 1.6).

Figure 1.6: Perceptions of Difficulty in Finding a Job in Yucatán, Now *vs.* Five Years Ago

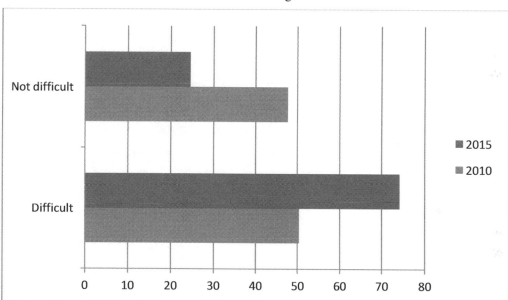

---

[18] The Mexican government's social welfare programs do not perform flawlessly. For example, Carmen, a 48-year-old housewife in Tunkás, expressed a sense of disdain for the Prospera program. She explained that her family had been getting by with the benefits from the program for a couple of years until they received a letter explaining that she and her family were no longer eligible to participate in the program. She was baffled by the letter and claims that none of her qualifications had changed since her family began to receive benefits.

Many of our interviewees explained this difficulty by citing their lack of a high school diploma, which is now required by many employers in the service industry. As Francisco, a 57-year-old Tunkaseño currently living in Yucatán's state capital, explained: "In Mérida there are better jobs as long as you are educated. Since I was young I looked for opportunities to prepare myself in Mexico professionally. As a well prepared person, I was able to find employment that satisfies all of my needs in Mexico." Similarly, Jorge reported: "To get a good job you need to get a degree, because they ask you for diplomas. Someone who doesn't finish their studies or who only finishes high school can only work in construction or in the fields. That barely lets you provide for your family." This conundrum is further highlighted by the fact that most Tunkaseños who have never migrated are housewives (49.3 percent), work in agriculture (13.4 percent), and/or work in non-professional service jobs (11.9 percent).

It is interesting that while pessimism about the state of the Mexican labor market is widespread among Tunkaseños, this view was held most strongly by complete non-migrants. Only 5.2 percent of this group reported that it was easier to get a job in Mexico currently than five years ago. This may be due to the fact that non-migrants rely solely on the local, Tunkás labor market, which has been contracting for decades and contrasts sharply with that of the Yucatán peninsula overall (Gell-Redman, et al., 2010: 106). Tunkaseños with only internal migration experience had a somewhat positive view of the Mexican labor market (15.2 percent), when compared to other groups. The optimism of internal migrants might be explained by their higher level of education: Internal migrants have more education than any other group of interviewees, averaging 10.4 years of formal education. This gives them better access to jobs in tourist cities on the Yucatán peninsula. Finally, when comparing Tunkaseños with low- and high- propensity to migrate internationally, their evaluations of the labor market in Mexico are as expected. Low-propensity migrants are more optimistic about the Mexican labor market then high-propensity migrants; 15.9 percent of the former group agreed that it is easier to find a job in Mexico today compared to five years ago, while 12.6 percent of the latter group thought so.

Tunkás remains a place where low-end poverty remains extensive. Programs like Prospera and Seguro Popular put more family members into the health care and education systems, which directly and indirectly builds their human capital. But overall views of the Mexican labor market remain pessimistic. Social welfare programs may not be anything more than a buffer of survival for those who are severely impoverished, and thus unable to migrate domestically or internationally. The heavy weight of the depressed agricultural sector in the local economy may explain the difficulty that many residents perceive in finding a job (without leaving the town). Taken together, these findings suggest that while national macroeconomic trends point to improved labor market conditions, this trend has not been experienced by residents of places like Tunkás. Thus, it is unlikely that better economic conditions in Mexico have shaped Tunkaseños' decisions to stay home rather than migrate to the United States.

Migration to Destinations in Mexico as a Substitute for International Migration

Two-thirds of our interviewees in Tunkás reported that they had never sought work within Mexico, outside of Tunkás. Nevertheless, Tunkaseños' lifetime rate of internal migration (33 percent) is higher than their participation in international migration (22.4 percent). Moreover, data from migration histories show a sharp increase in migration to destinations within Mexico in recent years (see Figure 1.7). The most popular domestic destinations for Tunkaseños were Cancún (46.4 percent), Mérida (22.3 percent), and Playa del Carmen, another resort city (14.5 percent). Commuting to jobs in these nearby cities, rather than leaving Tunkás permanently, was the preferred option of 15.6 percent of our Tunkás-based interviewees in 2015.

Figure 1.7: Internal Migration from Tunkás, by Year of Most Recent Departure

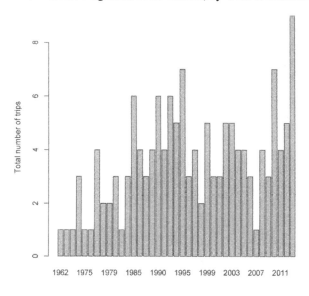

27

The attractiveness of internal migration was evident in Tunkaseños' plans for the next 12 months. More than one out of ten (10.9 percent) of our interviewees reported that they intended to migrate internally during calendar year 2015, compared with just 2.5 percent who were planning to go to the United States. Our data show that the majority of Tunkaseños who have some international migration experience had no history of internal migration (56.7 percent), but 43.3 percent had both internal and international migration histories. These findings lend support to the hypothesis that internal migration is serving as a substitute for international migration for some Tunkaseños, despite the increased difficulty in finding work in the Yucatán Peninsula that they perceive in recent years (see Figure 1.6 above). While most internal migrants work in non-professional services (44.4 percent) and construction (12.3 percent), it is important to note that many of them work in the professional service sector (16.1 percent) – an increase of 8 percentage points from our 2012 survey in the town. This is consistent with the fact that internal migrants have the highest level of educational attainment among our interviewees. Internal migrants have been working as lawyers, psychologists, doctors, teachers, and skilled mechanics. For example, Francisco, a Tunkaseño who currently lives in Mérida, was able to find much better employment through internal migration: "I am an elementary school teacher. I have advanced degrees in educational psychology and clinical psychology, which gave me many occupational opportunities."

Tunkaseños recognize that wages offered by employers in their hometown are not sufficient to provide a decent living for them and their families. Nearly three-quarters (74 percent) believed that in Tunkás it is not possible to earn the equivalent of two minimum wages (132.9 pesos a day, or USD $8.50, as of January 2015). As Valeria put it: "At least [in Cancún] there are stable jobs. Here in Tunkás there are almost no jobs, and if there are, they're only in construction." Interviewees also mentioned that while wages in other parts of Mexico are not optimal, they are certainly higher than in Tunkás. However, when we examine what drives people to migrate internally, family ties seem more important than expected wages. When asked why they preferred to migrate to another locality in Mexico instead of going to the United States, a plurality of our interviewees responded that most of their family and friends did not live in the United States (29.5 percent), followed by a preference for the way of life in Mexico versus life in the United States (12.7 percent). Another common explanation was the perception that it is easier to get a job in Mexico than in the United States (12.2 percent).

In summary, our field data support the hypothesis that many potential migrants in Tunkás may be choosing destinations within Mexico rather than migrating to the United States. They choose internal migration because it lessens the emotional stress of long separations from their immediate relatives, they face fewer dangers in migrating within Mexico, they do not live in fear from a lack of legal status in the United States, and they are able to find a job that pays at least two minimum wages without leaving the Yucatán Peninsula. As Toña, a 40-year-old interviewee, told us: "Here in Tunkás you live a peaceful life, but there is no money. However, if you go north without documents you always live with the fear of being deported."

Family Ties That Bind

Family ties seem to be the single most important reason why people stay in Tunkás, as well as why some return home from the United States. Among our interviewees who reported that they were not planning to migrate to the United States in 2015, a plurality (33.7 percent) said that they were staying in Mexico because most of their family members reside there. Moreover, as shown in Figure 1.8, more than two-thirds (69.1 percent) of those who have returned to Tunkás to live (not just visit briefly) did so because of family-related issues, such as family emergencies and funerals. Such was the case of Toña, who explained that she returned to Mexico because her mother and father were ill, her mother with advanced diabetes. She felt it was her responsibility to take care of them. She also confessed that she missed her family a lot, even though some of her cousins were also living in the United States.

Figure 1.8: Most Important Reason for Returning from the U.S. to Live in Mexico

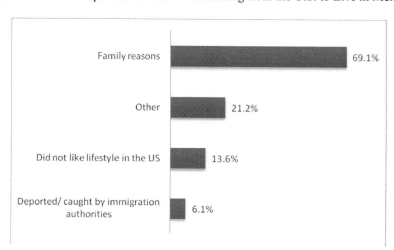

29

Aside from illness, family obligations were also an important factor in Tunkaseños' decisions to return. This was true for Daniel: "My dad was working here alone and he needed me to help him out, so I came back." But many returnees simply missed their family in Mexico. That was the case of Valeria's husband: "[My husband] spent three years in the United States. Once he got back he said, 'I'm not going back,' because in three years he didn't see his son."

On the other hand, as reported above, the second most important reason for Tunkaseños going to the United States on their most recent trip was to reunite with family members already living in that country (20.5 percent). Interviewees who have a high propensity to migrate to the United States have an average of 1.4 relatives there (including a spouse, children, siblings, parents, and grandparents), while those with low propensity to go north have 0.6 relatives living abroad. Internal migrants have the lowest number of U.S.-based relatives (0.2). If we examine relatives in Mexico, the picture is almost completely reversed: Complete non-migrants have a median of 9 family members in Mexico, internal migrants have 8.3 relatives there, those with low propensity to migrate internationally have 8.7 relatives in Mexico, and those with a high propensity to migrate to the United States have the lowest number of relatives in Mexico (7.8).

In sum, family ties pull Tunkaseños in both directions. For some potential migrants, such ties anchor them strongly in the home community. For others, they serve as an incentive for migrating to the United States. Return migrants from the United States also seem to have been strongly influenced by family ties. Previous MMFRP research has demonstrated that returnees have weaker social networks in the United States than those who have settled there. Their relative lack of social ties to the United States, coupled with a desire for family reunification, motivates their decision to return to Mexico (Kosnac et al., 2013: 41).

It is also important to note that there is a clear gender difference among stay-at-homes in Tunkás: Women predominate among complete non-migrants and persons with low propensity to migrate internationally. Although Tunkaseña women have started to migrate at higher rates than in the past, it is still common practice for the husband to migrate first, leaving their spouse and children in Mexico. Among our 2015 interviewees, 42.7 percent reported that they left their children in Mexico during their most recent trip to the United States, mostly (77.6 percent) in their mother's care. On the other hand, a woman with a spouse in the United States is more likely to migrate there, thus reunifying the family on that side of the border.

PROPENSITY TO MIGRATE TO THE UNITED STATES: A MULTIVARIATE ANALYSIS

To assess the relative importance of the factors that may discourage migration to the United States, we created two ordinary least squares multivariate regression models. As the dependent variable for both models we used our summative index of propensity to migrate internationally. As described above, this index summarizes information about an interviewee's prior migration history (e.g., having ever migrated to the United States, the number of trips in the last five years), the total amount of time he/she has spent in the United States (normalized to preserve scale), whether the respondent intends to migrate in the next 12 months, and whether or not he/she is of prime migration age, which we define as being 18-35 years old.

To measure the effects of our seven hypothesized migration discouragement factors we used 2-3 independent variables per factor. Macro-level data suggest that the U.S. low-skilled job market has been slowly recovering from the Great Recession but has not yet returned to pre-Recession conditions. To test the effects of weaker labor demand in the United States we created a variable for having lost one's job or suffered reduced work hours (underemployment within the past twelve months. A second variable measures the perceived difficulty of finding employment in the United States during the last five years.

To test the effects of stronger U.S. immigration enforcement, we used three independent variables. The first measures the respondent's perception of increased difficulty in crossing the border without papers now, as compared to five years ago. The second variable is knowledge of someone who has been deported from the United States within the last five years. Our third variable measures whether the interviewee perceives a change in the volume of deportations from the United States over the past five years.

In relation to remote deterrence, our first variable tests if respondents think that crossing the border is more dangerous now, compared to five years ago. Second, we test the effect of knowing someone who was killed or kidnapped while crossing the border without authorization.

To assess the impact of changes in the people-smuggling industry, we included one independent variable in our model. Following the argument that people-smuggling operations are now being run by larger, semi-autonomous organizations that are more likely to have criminal ties, we constructed a variable that tests whether people believe *polleros* have more contact with criminal organizations now than in the past.

The effect of improved labor market and living conditions in Mexico is tested using two independent variables. First, we created a dichotomous variable for people receiving benefits from government social welfare programs such as PROCAMPO, PROGAN,[19] Seguro Popular, and Prospera. Our second variable measures Mexican labor market conditions by asking if the respondent believes it was easier to find a job within Mexico in 2015 than in 2010.

To address internal migration as a substitute for international migration we used three variables. Our first variable asks if a respondent has any history of migration to a Mexican destination for employment. Next we measure the intention to migrate within the Yucatán Peninsula in the next twelve months. Our final variable measures whether respondents thought they were more likely to find a job that pays at least two minimum wages elsewhere in the Yucatán Peninsula than in Tunkás.

The effect of family ties with the United States was measured by the number of relatives the respondent has who are currently living in the United States, including spouses, parents, grandparents, siblings, and children. Model 2 also includes a variable to measure the relationship between propensity to migrate internationally and the number of one's relatives who live in Mexico. In both models we used gender and education as control variables. The results of our multivariate analyses are reported in Table 1.2.

---

[19]A program that incentivizes cattle breeders to use green technologies that improve management of natural resources in their sector.

Table 1.2: Multivariate Analysis of Propensity to Migrate to the U.S.
(coefficients; standard errors in parentheses)

	Model 1	Model 2
Experienced lay off or cut in work hours	0.019 (0.112)	0.027 (0.112)
Perception that it is hard to get a job in U.S.	0.139 (0.114)	0.139 (0.114)
Perception of difficulty in crossing border	0.059 (0.131)	0.060 (0.131)
Know someone who was deported	0.122 (0.135)	0.112 (0.135)
Thinks that deportations have risen in last 5 years	**0.258*** (0.114)	**0.255*** (0.114)
Knows someone who was kidnaped or died at the border	-0.095 (0.113)	-0.100 (0.113)
Perception that crossing border is dangerous	0.014 (0.130)	0.019 (0.130)
Believes that polleros are involved with organized crime	-0.209 (0.187)	-0.191 (0.188)
Household participates in government welfare programs	-0.167 (0.215)	-0.179 (0.215)
Perception that it is easy to get a job in Mexico	0.011 (0.150)	0.017 (0.150)
Has internal migration history	0.094 (0.116)	0.094 (0.116)
Intends to migrate internally in next year	0.016) (0.151)	0.025 (0.151)
Optimistic about getting better job in Yucatán Peninsula	0.083 (0.109)	0.079 (0.109)
Number of relatives in the United States	**0.195*** (0.040)	**0.204*** (0.041)
Number of relatives in Mexico	-----	0.016 (0.016)
Male	**0.628*** (0.111)	**0.635*** (0.111)
Education	-0.001 (0.013)	0.002 (0.013)
Constant	0.359 (0.328)	0.179 (0.371)
N	331	331
R^2	0.220	0.222

Significance: *p< .05; **p <.01; ***p<.001.

33

Aside from gender (males have a higher propensity to migrate internationally), the only two significant predictors in our models are (1) the belief that deportations of Mexican migrants from the United States have increased in number in the past five years, and (2) the respondent's number of relatives living in the United States. Both variables are statistically significant at close to, or above, the alpha = .01 level, and the F-statistic strongly rejects the null hypothesis that the independent variables are jointly insignificant. The adjusted R-squared statistic is high for this type of data (over .2). In other words, these findings are quite robust. The addition of the respondent's number of relatives in Mexico in our second model has virtually no effect on the overall results.

It is counter-intuitive that believing that deportations of migrants from the United States have increased in recent years makes one more likely to migrate internationally. There are at least two possible explanations. First, we hypothesize that knowledge of deportation dynamics is also measuring the respondent's degree of connection to the United States. Knowledge of the large number deportations occurring during the Obama presidency is associated with a higher degree of U.S.-connectedness, which is the underlying predictor of propensity to migrate to the United States. Alternatively, the relationship may be explained by the fact that people planning to migrate are likely to be better informed about immigration issues in general and therefore are more likely to have heard about large-scale deportations. This finding is consistent with previous MMFRP research on migration from Tunkás, which found that knowledge about the consequences of U.S. immigration control measures was positively, not negatively, related to intent to migrate to the United States (Hicken *et al.* 2009: 86-87).

Our multivariate analysis shows that people are significantly more likely to migrate internationally if they have larger numbers of relatives living in the United States. However, the relationship is moderately weak, with a coefficient of 0.195 in the first model and 0.204 in the second. It is somewhat surprising that having large numbers of relatives in Mexico proved to be non-significant, given that most of our interviewees cited family matters as the most important reason for staying put or returning to Tunkás from the United States. A possible explanation is that, while most of our interviewees have fewer relatives in the United States than in Mexico, it is possible that having a key relative, such as a spouse or a child, living in the United States might have a stronger influence on migration propensity than having parents, grandparents, or siblings in Mexico. Nonetheless, our results are generally consistent with theories of migration that emphasize the importance of social networks operating in the migrant-receiving country (e.g., Massey 1998; McKeown 1999). Despite the fact that Tunkás is a relatively recent community of emigration, the social networks linking it to the United States appear to be mature and influential in decisions to migrate.

Another important negative finding of our multivariate analysis is that the relationship between U.S. labor market conditions and propensity to migrate is statistically insignificant. All of the independent variables measuring U.S. labor market conditions are positively related to migration propensity but none of them are statistically significant predictors. This finding is unexpected, given previous research suggesting that Mexican migration to the United States is fundamentally driven by employment and wage differentials. We would expect potential migrants to be more strongly influenced by labor conditions in the United States. Moreover, as noted above, a majority of our interviewees (50.8 percent) stated that economic considerations were what motivated them most strongly to make their most recent trip to the United States. The most likely explanation for the lack of statistical significance of U.S. labor market conditions in our multivariate model is that most Tunkaseños who go to the United States work in service jobs which were relatively unaffected by the Great Recession.

While the frequency of internal migration from Tunkás seems to have increased in recent years while as migration to the United States contracted sharply, we find that intention to migrate to a Mexican destination during 2015 was not a significant predictor of propensity to migrate internationally. The same was true for our "remote deterrence" variables. More than one in ten of our interviewees believed that it was "very dangerous" to cross the border clandestinely. However, the relationship between perceived danger and propensity to migrate to the United States proved insignificant in our multivariate models. (If anything, people who perceive such danger are actually *more* likely to migrate to the United States.). Knowing someone who was kidnapped or died in a clandestine border crossing makes one less likely to migrate but is not statistically significant. Finally, believing that people-smugglers are involved with organized crime reduces one's propensity to migrate but is not a significant predictor.

To summarize, variables intended to measure the effects of macro-economic conditions in both Mexico and the United States proved to be non-significant, as were variables measuring the perceived difficulty and danger associated with clandestine border crossings. Previous MMFRP research also found that border enforcement policies

35

and perceptions of elevated border-crossing risks do not significantly influence the decision to migrate. But the perception among our 2015 interviewees that more people are getting deported from the United States did prove to be a significant predictor -- though not as a discouragement factor. People who know that deportations have been rising are actually *more* likely to migrate to the United States. The strength of one's social network in the United States was a highly significant predictor of international migration propensity. The lack of statistical significance for family connections in Mexico might be due to the fact that our measure masks the importance of key relatives such as parents or a spouse.

CONCLUSION

This chapter adopted a novel analytic perspective on recent Mexico-to-U.S. migration trends. Instead of trying to explain why people are migrating to the United States, we focused on identifying the factors that influence potential migrants to stay home in Mexico, in the aftermath of the Great Recession.

In regard to U.S. border enforcement as a migration-discouraging factor, we found that awareness of the danger and difficulty of clandestine border crossings, as well as the belief that deportations from the United States have increased in the last five years, do influence one's propensity to migrate internationally, but not in the expected way. Holding such beliefs and perceptions actually seems to make one more likely to go north, not less. These counter-intuitive findings confirm results from three previous MMFRP surveys, conducted in different years and different parts of Mexico. The explanation may lie in better information, obtained particularly from U.S.-based relatives and friends. We found that interviewees with a high propensity to migrate to the United States have the strongest social networks in that country.

We also considered changes in the people-smuggling industry as another possible discouragement factor for potential migrants. We found that the vast majority of people in our research community – more than 80 percent -- believe that there is a growing connection between professional people-smugglers and organized crime in Mexico, regardless of the interviewee's propensity to migrate. This belief have pushed up the fees that can be charged by people-smugglers located through relatives or friends – what might be called a "vetting premium." But regardless of how *polleros* are hired, the safety or danger of placing oneself in their hands does not seem to vary: 96.7 percent of our interviewees reported that the *pollero* they hired most recently had made good on his

36

commitments.

The flow of migrants from Tunkás to cities within Mexico has increased considerably in recent years, even as migration to the United States has fallen sharply. We found mixed evidence on the relationship between internal and international migration behavior. Some of our quantitative and qualitative data support the notion that more potential migrants are choosing destinations within Mexico because it lessens psychological stressors associated with migration to the United States. In our multivariate analysis, having internal migration experience is positively related to one's propensity to migrate to the United States, perhaps because internal migration serves as a "school" for international migration, but is not a statistically significant predictor.

Social connectivity with the United States is what seems to drive most northbound migration, according to our multivariate analysis. We found that the number of U.S.-based relatives is the most potent predictor of propensity to migrate internationally. By the same token, a lack of social connectivity – having few relatives or other social network contacts in the United States – is what anchors stay-at-homes most strongly. Whether in the form of relatives who pull prospective migrants to one destination or the other, or the information they give potential migrants about immigration enforcement in the United States, or through the connections they provide for finding a job or hiring a people-smuggler, social network contacts are crucial.

Previous MMFRP field studies suggest another reason why so few Tunkaseños (and other would-be Mexican migrants) are now contemplating migration to the United States: People who had the highest propensity to migrate have already gone north. And most of those who left for the United States during the last ten years or so have stayed there, at least in part because of the caging effect of tighter border enforcement (García & Barreno, 2007; López et al., 2007; Kosnac, et al., 2013). Thus, the pool of potential migrants in Tunkás and other Mexican rural communities with a history of sending people to the United States is smaller today than ever before.[20] Those who remain in Tunkás are mostly those who have the fewest social network contacts in the United States. They are likely to have a lower propensity to migrate internationally than those who left in previous years, especially in the 1990s, and they tend to be focused on employment opportunities in Yucatán rather than the United States. This is reflected in

---

[20] The declining birth rate in Mexico has also reduced the pool of potential migrants (National Research Council, 2011: 36-38; Chishti & Hipsman 2015).

37

the recent increase in migration to destinations within Mexico.

What effect did the Great Recession in the United States have on migration flows? We found that few residents of our research community in Yucatán, as well as members of the town's satellite communities in southern California, had been seriously damaged by the U.S. economic crisis. For example, only 8.9 percent of our Mexico-based interviewees had returned from the United States because of unemployment or under-employment in that country. By contrast, three-quarters of our respondents, on both sides of the border, had a pessimistic view of the labor market in Mexico.

As noted above, the total stock of Mexican undocumented immigrants in the U.S. has declined by about 1 million since the pre-Great Recession peak in 2007. But the magnitude of the decline is considerably less than might have been expected, considering the severity of the recession. If the border had been more porous when the recession hit (i.e., less intensively patrolled, with lower fees being charged by people-smugglers), almost certainly more migrants would have retuned to Mexico. Instead, most Mexican undocumented migrants dug in as the Great Recession hit, coped with it as best they could, and continued to live and work in the United States. They developed new income-earning strategies, put more family members into the U.S. work force, and reduced the remittances they were sending to relatives in Mexico.[21] Moreover, Tunkaseños already in the United States when the Great Recession hit were relatively insulated from its effects because most were employed in services rather than construction and other recession-sensitive sectors, so there was no economic incentive to return home.

In sum, why are so many of today's potential migrants deciding to stay home rather than leave for the United States? Our findings suggest that social factors (e.g., family obligations, the locus and density of social network contacts) are more important to them than labor market conditions and restrictive U.S. immigration policies. Many Tunkaseños seem to be seeking better-paid employment in the Yucatán Peninsula, despite the perceived difficulty of finding jobs there. They seem less willing than the preceding generation of Tunkasenos to venture off to a foreign country, paying thousands of dollars to a people-smuggler, possibly facing life-threatening hazards en route, having to navigate a new language and strange customs, in a place where they would not be able to count on much support from family and friends as they try to start a new life. This is the new calculus of staying home in Mexico.

---

[21] For more information about Tunkaseño coping strategies and the effects of the economic crisis in Tunkaseño employment, see Aguilar et al. (2010).

REFERENCES CITED

Aguilar, A., Harman, G., Keyes, D., Markman, L., & Matus, M. (2010). Coping with *la crisis*. Pp. 15-45 in W. Cornelius, D. Fitzgerald, P. Lewin-Fischer, & L. Muse-Orlinoff, eds. (2010) *Mexican Migration and the U.S. Economic Crisis, A Transnational Perspective*. La Jolla, CA: Center for Comparative Immigration Studies, University of California-San Diego.

Andreas, P. (2001). The transformation of migrant smuggling across the U.S.-Mexican border. In Kyle, D. & Koslowski, R., eds., *Global Human Smuggling: Comparative Perspectives*. Baltimore, MD: Johns Hopkins University Press.

Bacon, D. (2013). *The Right to Stay Home: How U.S. policy Drives Mexican Migration*. Boston: Beacon Press.

Castillo, G., Jiménez-Pacheco, Z., and Pasillas, P. (2007). Stay-at-homes: Why many people do not migrate. Pp. 141-49 in Cornelius, W., Fitzgerald, D., & Lewin-Fischer, P., eds., *Mayan Journeys: The New Migration from Yucatán to the United States*. La Jolla, CA: Center for Comparative Immigration Studies, University of California, San Diego.

Chishti, M. & Hipsman F. (2015). In historic shift, new migration flows from Mexico fall below those from China and India. *Migration Policy Institute*. Retrieved from http://www.migrationpolicy.org/article/historic-shift-new-migration-flows-mexico-fall-below-those-china-and-india.

Cornelius, W. (2001). Death at the border: Efficacy and unintended consequences of U.S. immigration control policy. *Population and Development Review, 27*(4): 661-685.

Cornelius, W. (2005). Controlling 'unwanted' migration: Lessons from the United States, 1993-2004. *Journal of Ethnic and Migration Studies*, 31(4): 775-94.

Cornelius, W., & Salehyan, I. (2007). Does border enforcement deter unauthorized immigration? The case of Mexican migration to the United States of America. *Regulation & Governance*, 1(2): 139-153.

Davis B., Stecklov G., & Winters P. (2002). Domestic and international migration from rural Mexico: Disaggregating the effects of network structure and composition. *Population Studies,* 56 (3): 291-309.

De León, J. (2012) "Better to be host than caught": Excavating the conflicting roles of migrant material culture." American Anthropologist, 114(3): 477-95. doi: 10.1111/j.1548-1433.2012.01447.x

Eyzaguirre, N. (2011). Sustaining Latin America's transformation. *Finance and Development*, 48 (1): 9-12.

Fischbein, J., Malabad, K., Acosta, S., Dueñas, C., & Velasco Viloria, I. (2013). U.S. border enforcement in an era of economic uncertainty: The limits of deterrence and legal alternatives. Pp. 19-39 in FitzGerald, D., Hernández Díaz, J., & Keyes, D., eds., *The Wall Between Us: A Mixteco Migrant Community in Mexico and the United States.* La Jolla, CA: Center for Comparative Immigration Studies, University of California, San Diego.

FitzGerald, D. & Alarcón, R. (2013). Migration: Policies and politics. Pp. 111-38 in Smith, P., & Selee, A., eds., *Mexico and the United States: The Politics of Partnership.* Boulder, CO: Lynne Rienner Publishers.

Fuentes, J. & Garcia, O. (2009). *Coyotaje:* The structure and the functioning of the people-smuggling industry. Pp. 79-100 in Cornelius, W., FitzGerald, D., & Borger, S., eds., *Four Generations of Norteños: New Research from the Cradle of Mexican Migration.* La Jolla, CA: Center for Comparative Immigration Studies, University of California, San Diego.

Galván, A. (2014). Border deaths drop to 15-year low. *The Huffington Post,* October 27. Retrieved from: http://www.huffingtonpost.com/2014/10/27/border-deaths-drop_n_6053952.html.

García, A. (2014). Hidden in plain sight: How unauthorized migrants strategically assimilate in restrictive localities in California. *Journal of Ethnic and Migration Studies* (February). doi:10.1080/1369183X.2014.883918.

García, A., & Barreno, A. (2007). Tunkaseño settlement in the United States. Pp. 115-39 in Cornelius, W., FitzGerald, D., & Lewin-Fischer, P., eds., *Mayan Journeys: The New Migration from Yucatán to the United States.* La Jolla, CA: Center for Comparative Immigration Studies, University of California, San Diego.

Gell-Redman, M.; Andrade, E., Martell, A.; & Jimenez Pacheco Z. (2010). Inhabiting two worlds: Tunkaseños in the transnational labor market. Pp. 105-29 in Cornelius, W., FitzGerald, D., Lewin-Fischer, P., & Muse-Orlinoff, L., eds., *Mexican Migration and the U.S. Economic crisis, A Transnational Perspective.* La Jolla, CA: Center for Comparative Immigration Studies, University of California-San Diego.

González-Barrera, A., & Krogstad, J. (2015). What we know about illegal immigration from Mexico. Pew Research Center, Washington, D.C., FactTank, July 15. Retrieved from: http://www.pewresearch.org/fact-tank/2015/07/15/what-we-know-about-illegal-immigration-from-mexico/

Hanson, G. (2009). The economics and policy of illegal immigration in the United States. Migration Policy Institute, Washington, D.C., Research Reports, December: 1-16.

Hicken, J., Cohen, M., & Narvaez, J. (2010). Double jeopardy: How U.S. enforcement policies shape Tunkaseño migration. Pp. 47-92 in Cornelius, W., FitzGerald, D., Lewin-Fischer, P., Muse-Orlinoff, L., eds., *Mexican Migration and the U.S. Economic Crisis: A Transnational Perspective.* La Jolla, CA: Center for Comparative Immigration Studies, University of California-San Diego.

Hicken, J., Fishbein, J., & Lisle, J. (2011). U.S. border enforcement: The limits of physical and remote deterrence of unauthorized migration." Pp. 17-35 in FitzGerald, D., Alarcón, R., & Muse-Orlinoff, L., eds., *Recession Without Borders: Mexican Migrants Confront the Economic Downturn.* La Jolla, CA: Center for Comparative Immigration Studies, University of California, San Diego.

Kaye, J. (2010) *Moving Millions: How Coyote Capitalism Fuels Global Immigration.* New York: Wiley.

Kochhar, R. (2014). Latino jobs growth driven by U.S.-born: Immigrants no longer the majority of hispanic workers. Pew Research Center, Washington, D.C., Hispanic Trends Project, June 19.

Kosnac, H., Mejorado, Y., Davidson, S., Marroquín, M., & Nazario, C. (2013). To settle or to return? What matters most in migrants' decisions. Pp. 31-72 in Cornelius, W., Lizardi-Gómez, A., Van Vooren, A., & Keyes, D., eds., *Return Migration, Health, and Sexuality in a Transnational Mexican Community.* Guadalajara, Mexico, and La Jolla, CA: Universidad de Guadalajara and Center for Comparative Immigration Studies, University of California, San Diego.

López, H., Oliphant, R., & Tejeda, E. (2007). U.S. settlement behavior and labor market participation. Pp. 75-96 in Cornelius, W., & Lewis, J., eds., *Impacts of Border Enforcement on Mexican Migration.* La Jolla, CA: Center for Comparative Immigration Studies, University of California, San Diego.

López Castro, G. (1998). Factors that influence migration: coyotes and alien smuggling. Pp. 965-74 in vol. 3, *Mexico-U.S. Binational Migration Study.* Mexico, DF, and Washington, DC: Mexican Ministry of Foreign Relations and U.S. Commission on Immigration Reform.

Martin, P., & Abella, M. (2006). *Managing Labor Migration in the Twenty-first Century.* New Haven, CT: Yale University Press.

Massey, D., Arango, J., Hugo, G., Kouaouci, A., Pellegrino, A., & Taylor, J. (1993). Theories of international migration: A review and appraisal." *Population and Development Review,* 19 (3): 431-66.

Massey, D., & International Union for the Scientific Study of Population (1998). *Worlds in motion: Understanding International Migration at the End of the Millennium.* Oxford: Clarendon Press.

McKeown, A. (1999). Transnational Chinese families and Chinese exclusion, 1875-1943. *Journal of American Ethnic History,* 18 (2): 73-110.

Muse-Orlinoff, L. & Lewin Fisher, P. (2010). Introduction. Pp. 1-14 in Cornelius, W., FitzGerald, D., Lewin-Fischer, P., & Muse-Orlinoff, L., eds., *Mexican Migration and the U.S. Economic Crisis: A Transnational Perspective.* La Jolla, CA: Center for Comparative Immigration Studies, University of California, San Diego.

National Research Council (2011). *Budgeting for Immigration Enforcement: A Path to Better Performance.* Washington, DC: National Academies Press.

Olson, G. (2012). Felipe Calderón: empleo redujo migración. *Excélsior* (Mexico City), April 25.

Papademetriou, D., & Terrazas, A. (2009). Immigrants in the United States and the current economic crisis. Migration Policy Institute, Washington, D.C., *Migration Information Source*, April 1.

Passel, J. (2015). Testimony of Jeffrey S. Passel: Unauthorized immigrant population: National and state trends, industries, and occupations. Pew Hispanic Center, Washington, D.C., Hispanic Trends Project, March 26.

Passel, J., D'Vera C., & González-Barrera A. (2012). Net migration from Mexico falls to zero--and perhaps less. Pew Hispanic Center, Washington, D.C., April 23.

Preston, J. (2009). Mexican data show migration to U.S. in decline. *New York Times,* May 14.

Puentes, V., Hong, R., and Valencia R. (2011). Deciding to migrate. Pp. 63-73 in FitzGerald, D., Alarcón, R., & Muse-Orlinoff, L., eds., *Recession Without Borders: Mexican Migrants Confront the Economic Downturn.* La Jolla, CA: Center for Comparative Immigration Studies, University of California, San Diego.

Rios Contreras, V. (2014). The role of drug-related violence and extortion in promoting Mexican migration: Unexpected consequences of a drug war. *Latin American Research Review,* 49 (3): 199-217.

Rivero-Fuentes, E. (2005). Beyond income differentials: Explaining migrants' destinations in Mexico. Paper presented at the 25th International Population Conference, Tours, France, July 18. Retrieved from: http://demoscope.ru/weekly/knigi/tours_2005/papers/iussp2005s51591.pdf

Rodríguez, A., Wittlinger, J., & Manzanero Rodríguez, L. (2007). The interface between internal and international migration. Pp. 73-90 in Cornelius, W., FitzGerald, D., & Lewin-Fischer, P., eds.,*Mayan Journeys: The New Migration from Yucatán to the United States.* La Jolla, CA: Center for Comparative Immigration Studies, University of California, San Diego.

Saccheti, M. (2014). Searching for the unforgotten. Boston Globe, July 27.

Sen, A. (1999). *Development as Freedom*. New York: Knopf, 1999.

Silva, T., Niño, A., & Solís Lizama, M. (2007). Tunkás: A new community of emigration. Pp. 29-47 in Cornelius W., Fitzgerald D., & Lewin-Fischer, eds., *Mayan Journeys: U.S.-Bound Migration From a New Sending Community.* La Jolla, CA: Center for Comparative Immigration Studies, University of California, San Diego.

Spener, D. (2009). *Clandestine Crossings: Migrants and Coyotes on the Texas-Mexico Border.* Ithaca, NY: Cornell University Press.

Preparatoria students in Tunkás' Centro Bachillerato Tecnológico Agropecuario (CBTA).
(Photo by Rodrigo Díaz Guzmán)

2

Obstacles to Educational Attainment in a Transnational Community[22]

GABRIELA ESTRADA, SANDY GARCÍA, JESSICA HERNÁNDEZ, HILLARY KOSNAC, CELIA MEDINA, AND MICHELLE PLACERES

> I tell my son, "If you don't have an education nowadays, you won't be anything in this life. You aren't going to be able to survive on 20 or 30 pesos a day, working as a farmworker."
>
> *-- María Luisa, parent of a high school student in Tunkás*

In 2014, the Organisation for Economic Co-operation and Development (OECD) released a worrisome portrait of the Mexican education system. One of the most startling statistics was that among the 34 OECD countries, Mexico had the third lowest percentage of 15-19 year olds currently enrolled in school in 2012 (53 percent). Similarly, researchers at the RAND Corporation (Santibañez, et al. 2005) reported that average educational attainment among Mexicans 15 years of age or older was roughly eight years. Mexico also has a high teen-age pregnancy rate, which certainly undermines educational attainment (World Bank, 2015). Substance use and misuse among youth is also highly correlated with poor educational attainment (see, for example, National Center on Addiction and Substance Abuse at Columbia University, 2001).

Nevertheless, there have been some significant advances in the Mexican educational system. From 1950-2013, the mean number of years of schooling among adults 25 years or older in Mexico more than doubled, from 4 years to 8.5 years (United

---

[22]We thank Adam Sawyer for very helpful comments on an earlier version of this chapter.

Nations Development Programme, 2013). In less than a decade, adults in Mexico achieved an additional year of schooling, averaging 7.5 years in 2005 and 8.5 years in 2013 (United States Development Programme, 2013).

In 1997, the government started a cash-transfer program, now called Prospera, designed to encourage families to keep their girls and boys in school (Coordinación Nacional de Prospera Programa de Inclusión Social, 2014a). Policies such as extending compulsory education to include preschool and, more recently, upper compulsory education are also significant steps to increase educational attainment among Mexican youth. However, simply expanding compulsory education does not guarantee increased attainment. Paat (2014:62) observes that "compulsory education cannot resolve difficulties and complications caused by personal disposition, familial influences, and community factors that impede academic progress in Mexican families and societies."

What factors explain low levels of educational attainment in Mexico? Previous research has found that looking at Mexico at the national level camouflages important regional differences in terms of education (see, for example, Santibañez, et al., 2005). Although Mier, Rocha and Rabell Romero (2003) found that there has been improvement in educational opportunities for children living in rural communities, they emphasized that such communities continue to confront major educational obstacles, such as low-end poverty and, in indigenous communities, language barriers.

Our study explores the factors that influence educational attainment in Tunkás, a high-emigration town located in the Yucatán Peninsula. Specifically, we examine the ways in which parental involvement, school and teacher quality, and international migration -- all variables that prior research has shown to be associated with educational outcomes -- influence a young Tunkaseño's educational attainment. In addition, we explore community views on alcohol and drug use among the town's adolescents and the effects of substance abuse on their educational attainment and life chances. Our work builds upon previous research on education in Tunkás conducted by the MMFRP (Silva, et al., 2010).

We find some encouraging indicators of progress that mirror what has been happening at the national level in Mexico: Tunkaseño youth not only are completing more years of education than ever before; they are also improving upon high school graduation rates compared with previous generations of Tunkaseños. Our study suggests that higher parental education and teacher expectations are having a positive influence on the educational attainment of young Tunkaseños. Nevertheless, we find that students in Tunkás continue to face serious obstacles, such as schooling costs, teen pregnancy, and substance abuse. We find that adolescent alcohol and drug use, a relatively new phenomenon in Tunkás, is causing growing concern among teachers and parents.

We begin with a review of the literature on the factors that influence educational attainment, with a special focus on parental involvement, school and teacher quality, and migration. We then describe the educational system in Mexico and Tunkás more specifically. Next, we focus on Tunkás-based interviewees between the ages of 15 and 35, exploring the influence of the just-mentioned factors on their educational attainment. Finally, we examine the continuing constraints on educational attainment, with specific attention to substance abuse among adolescents. We conclude with several proposals rooted in our data to increase educational attainment among Tunkaseño youth and to decrease their rate of alcohol and drug consumption.

LITERATURE REVIEW

Previous scholars have pointed out that the majority of the world's educational research is based on students in the United States, and they caution against generalizing U.S.-based findings to other countries' educational settings. For example, while research in the United States and other advanced industrial nations suggests a strong influence of family and student characteristics on one's educational outcomes, studies in developing nations find school and teacher quality to be of greater importance (Heyneman & Loxley, 1983; Palafox, Prawda & Velez, 1994). The present study attempts to account for both types of variables.

The Influence of School and Teacher Quality

Carillo (2009) has suggested that school quality is central to educational attainment among Mexican-Americans. School quality includes factors such as the adequacy of school facilities and the availability of resources. Mwamwenda and Mwamwenda (1987) found that students who attended schools with adequate numbers of classrooms, desks, and textbooks performed significantly better than those who did not attend such schools. Looking at other indicators of school quality, Kozol (2005) highlighted that poor sanitation, overcrowding, absence of basic supplies and disrepair in segregated schools had negative consequences on students' educational outcomes.

47

School quality also encompasses teacher quality. In their study of 29 high- and low-income countries, Heyneman and Loxley (1983) found that among developing nations like Mexico, variance in educational outcomes can be explained largely by differences in school and teacher quality.[23] In their study of primary schools in Mexico, Palafox, Prawda and Velez (1994) found a positive correlation between a state's level of educational development and the cognitive results of its students. Their measures of educational development included indicators of teacher quality such as teacher dedication throughout the school year, fewer teacher strikes (and a corresponding increase in school days), and better-trained teachers.

Other studies have measured teacher quality in a variety of ways. For example, Skinner and Belmont (1993) found that students' sense of competence and self-efficacy were shaped by teacher affection, dedication, and dependability. Other studies employ measures like certification, highest level of education, and years of experience in the classroom as proxies for teacher quality. A growing amount of research focuses on the influence of a teacher's expectations on students' educational attainment (Rosenthal & Jacobsen, 1968; Brophy, 2010). Teacher engagement and high expectations are important, especially in contexts where there may be limited parental involvement in education or insufficient resources for their children's education. This does not necessarily mean a student will seek higher education if he/she has a caring teacher, but it does mean that educators can positively or negatively influence students' attitudes toward education (OECD, 2015).

Parental Influence on Educational Attainment

Another line of research postulates that certain family characteristics (e.g., parents' level of education, their involvement and expectations) have a greater influence on student performance than the school and teachers. Various studies have found a strong, positive association between parental education and levels of academic success in high school students (Blair, Blair, & Madama, 1999; Tavani & Losh, 2003; Sandefur, et al., 2006). These studies have found a positive association between higher levels of parental education and increased parental resources, rates of participation in early

---

[23]Heyneman and Loxley (1983) found that in Mexico 55 percent of the explained achievement variance was a result of school and teacher quality.

childhood education programs, and home literacy activities (Bogenschneidcer, 1997; Bakker, Denessen, & Brus-Laeven, 2007).

Other studies have found that higher parental expectations have a positive effect on educational attainment. Researchers suggest that while social class is strongly related to educational goals, parental aspirations or parental encouragement of higher education can override the influence of socioeconomic factors (Bordua, 1960; Cohen, 1965; Ellis and Lane, 1963; Kahl, 1953; Rehberg and Westby, 1967; Strodtbeck, 1958). For example, Kandel and Lesser (1969) found that 82 percent of adolescents plan to continue their education beyond high school when a mother strongly encourages the pursuit of higher education, while only 14 percent plan to do so when the mother reported that she advised against college attendance.

The Influence of Migration on Educational Attainment

Another family-related factor that may shape a youth's educational trajectory is the migration of a parent. Prior research has found that parental migration can have conflicting effects on the education of a child who stays behind. McKenzie and Rapoport (2006) found that children from migrant households were less likely to attend school and they complete fewer total years of schooling than children from non-migrating families. Similarly, Halpcrn-Manners (2011) found that having migrant family members had a large, negative effect on both the educational attainment and labor force participation of non-migrant youth. It could be that increased household work resulting from an absent parent is a stressor that children of migrant families face more often than their counterparts. Working in a family business or doing housework become responsibilities that are more important than attending school.

Others have hypothesized that in high-migration communities, a "culture of migration" may emerge in which the youth with connections to the United States may be more likely to migrate rather than complete their schooling in Mexico (see, for example, Kandel & Massey, 2002; Kandel & Kao, 2001). However, research has suggested that the negative effects of migration can be lessened by a variety of factors. The actions of the parent who stays behind can help to encourage additional educational attainment. McKenzie and Rapoport (2006) found that in migrant households there was a positive relationship between the mother's level of education and the educational attainment of the child. Moreover, financial contributions by a migrant working abroad can enable non-migrant youth to increase their educational attainment. Nobles (2011) found a positive correlation between household remittances and the amount of education children completed. Similarly, Kandel and Kao (2001) found a positive relationship between academic performance and family-member migration. These findings support the notion that remittances help to defray educational costs and, more broadly, household costs that may influence a young person's decision to begin working instead of studying. Nevertheless, other research has found no support for a "remittance effect" on educational attainment (Sawyer, 2014: 29).

EDUCATIONAL CONTEXT
Education in Mexico

The Mexican educational system consists of four basic levels: pre-school, compulsory basic education, upper secondary education, and higher education. Compulsory basic education refers to elementary, or *primaria*, which encompasses first through sixth grade, and middle school, or *secundaria*, which includes seventh through ninth grades. Upper secondary education, or *preparatoria*, is composed of grades tenth, eleventh and twelfth. As noted above, Mexicans over age 15 complete an average of eight years of schooling (Santibañez, et al., 2005). This translates into nearly completing a middle school education. By contrast, the mean number of years of schooling for adults over 25 years of age in the United States is 12.9 (United Nations Development Programme, 2013).

In addition to comparatively low levels of educational attainment, Mexico is also plagued by an illiteracy rate that has remained at roughly the same level for the past decade. Rojas (2014) found that about 6.8 percent of the population over age 15 is illiterate, meaning that about 5.8 million Mexicans can neither read nor write. This rate varies regionally: 18.4 percent of Chiapas' population is illiterate compared to less than 3 percent in Mexico City. There are also major differences by gender: 60 percent of Mexicans who are illiterate are female. Rojas quotes Hugo Casanova Cardiel, of the Universidad Nacional Autónoma de México (UNAM), on the consequences of Mexico's illiteracy problem: "[Being illiterate] creates marginalization; furthermore, illiteracy is concentrated in vulnerable populations like women, the indigenous, or those who are economically disadvantaged" (Rojas, 2014, para. 3).

Education in Tunkás

Tunkás has schools that serve students from pre-school to high school (upper secondary). These include two kindergartens, four elementary schools, one of which is a multi-grade school,[24] one technical middle school, and one technical high school. One of the kindergartens and one of the elementary schools are bilingual schools, teaching Maya as part of their curriculum. The middle school and high school (El Centro de Bachillerato Tecnológico Agropecuario, or CBTA) have a curricular focus on agriculture and computer systems.

The CBTA serves approximately 300 high school-age students from Tunkás and others who commute from neighboring municipalities. In addition, the CBTA offers an adult school program on Saturdays, designed to help those who left school finish their high school education. There are also options for adults who did not finish primary school and middle school. These options are offered through *escuelas abiertas*, where students largely complete their studies at home and only go to the school to take their exams.

With regard to higher education, Tunkás does not have a university or college branch. The closest universities are the Universidad Tecnológica del Centro and the Instituto de Educación Superior Excelencia y Humanismo (EXHUM), a private university. Both are located in Izamal—a thirty-minute commute from Tunkás. There are also opportunities for higher education in the state capital, Mérida, located two hours away.

EDUCATIONAL ATTAINMENT IN TUNKÁS

Overview

When we examine the educational attainment of Tunkaseños who were interviewed both in the town and in two southern California cities where Tunkaseño migrants are clustered, we find that Tunkaseños average a little over nine years of schooling. This finding is only slightly higher than the RAND Corporation's national estimate of an average of eight years of schooling among Mexicans 15 years and older

---

[24]"Felipe Carrillo Puerto" school is a primary, multi-grade school staffed by two teachers. One classroom serves grades first through third, while the other classroom serves fourth through sixth.

(Santibañez, et al., 2005). Not surprisingly, however, we find that our average varies dramatically by age cohort, as shown in Figure 2.1.

Figure 2.1: Educational Attainment of Tunkaseños, by Age Cohort

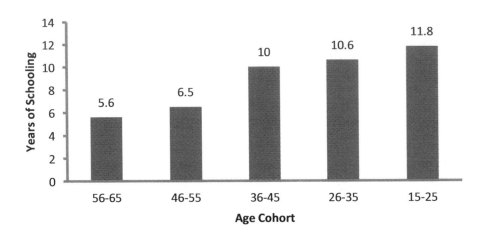

Younger Tunkaseños are completing more years of schooling than ever before. The average level of education of those 15 to 25 years old is almost 12 years of schooling, while the educational attainment of the oldest age cohort was roughly half (5.6 years).

It is important to note that these figures include Tunkaseños on both sides of the border. Figure 2.2 shows the differences in educational attainment of Tunkaseños based on place of residence. Generally, Mexico-based and U.S.-based Tunkaseños have similar levels of educational attainment. We find the biggest variation in years of schooling among those who fall into the 56-65 and 46-55 age cohorts. U.S.-based individuals in these cohorts average more than two additional years of education compared to their counterparts in Mexico. This difference could be attributed in part to the positive self-selection of Mexican migrants to the United States in terms of education. Previous research has noted that Mexican migrants to the United States are better educated than their non-migrant counterparts (Chiquiar & Hanson, 2005). We find that U.S.-based Tunkaseños in the younger age cohorts also have slightly higher levels of educational attainment compared to those living in Mexico. In both the 15-25 and 26-35 age groups, Tunkaseños living in the United States average less than a year more of schooling (0.4 and 0.2 more years, respectively).

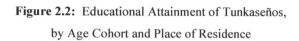

Figure 2.2: Educational Attainment of Tunkaseños,
by Age Cohort and Place of Residence

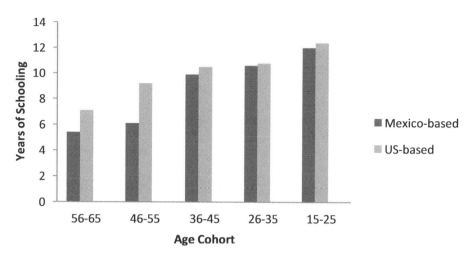

This pattern is generally consistent with previous research in Tunkás which found that younger Tunkaseños were advancing further in their educational pursuits than past generations (Silva, et al., 2010: 136). Nevertheless, Silva and his colleagues did not find evidence that the youngest cohort was able to improve upon the high school completion rate of the prior generation. For example, about 30 percent of both men and women in the 15-24 and the 25-34 age groups had completed their high school education. The authors cautioned that this finding could be an underestimate, because students who were still in school were included in their analysis.

In our analysis of those who have completed high school we excluded current students. This yielded a much different result than in Silva, et al. (2010). We find that the youngest generation has made impressive strides in terms of high school completion compared to previous generations. Figure 2.3 shows the percentage of Tunkaseños in each age cohort who have a high school diploma.[25] Two-thirds of Tunkaseños in the youngest age cohort have completed their high school education, almost doubling the percentage of their predecessors in the 26-35 age range (34.8 percent). This relatively recent increase in high school completion could be explained by a growing belief in the necessity of a high school education. Many Tunkaseños whom we interviewed asserted

---

[4]We coded those individuals who had completed technical or vocational training as the same as those with a high school diploma.

that it is essential for today's youth to complete their high school education in order for them to find employment.

Figure 2.3: High School Completion of Tunkaseños by Age Cohort[26]

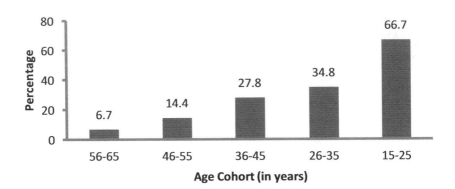

Elena, a mother and current student in Tunkás' adult school, reflected on the importance of completing high school:

> Right now, like in Cancún, if you don't have a high school diploma, they don't give you a job….Without a high-school education, they give you a low-level job where they pay you very little, but with a high school degree, you can get a better paying job.

In our interviews we found that this belief is widely held, not only by parents but among young Tunkaseños as well.

Despite the growing importance of a high school education and the substantial increase in Tunkaseños who have completed this level of schooling, we find that university attendance still remains low. Fewer than 10 percent of Tunkaseños in our sample have some degree of university-level education. Looking at specific age cohorts, only 6 percent of those between the ages of 15 and 25 have any level of university studies. This low proportion is likely a function of the age of those included in this cohort. We do find a higher proportion of individuals with some university education among 26-35 year olds (16.1 percent) and 36-45 year olds (14.2 percent). It is likely that

---

[26]We did not analyze high school graduation rates by place of residence, since the sample size for U.S.-based Tunkaseños became too small after excluding current students.

as time passes, a higher proportion of those in the 15-25 age group will have university-level studies, perhaps exceeding members of previous generations.

In fact, the majority of current students expressed a desire to pursue higher education. We asked these students about the level of education they would like to complete. Two-thirds of them indicated they would like to complete at least some college-level studies, with 59.8 percent saying they want to finish an undergraduate degree and 15.9 percent reporting a desire to complete an advanced degree. We also asked current students about the level of education they thought it was possible to finish. Figure 2.4 shows the discrepancies between what students would like to achieve and what they believe is possible.

Figure 2.4: Educational Aspirations versus Possible Educational Attainment

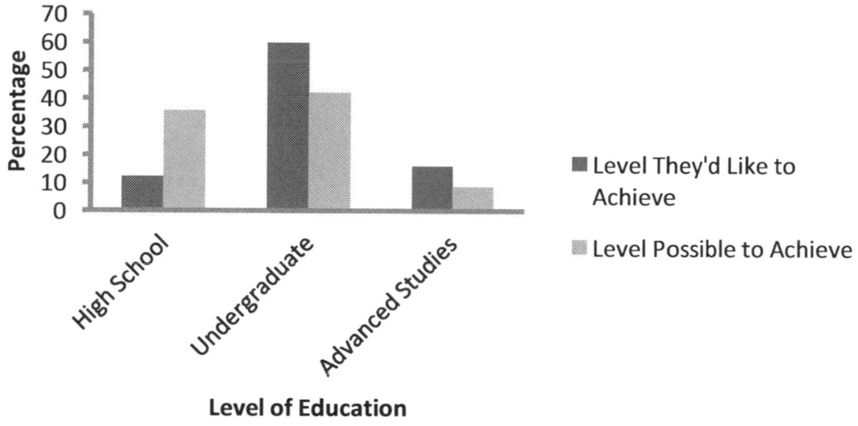

Overall, we find a marked difference between the level of education students desire to complete and what they believe is possible. This gap speaks to the existence of barriers that impede Tunkaseños from completing their desired level of education.

Mexico-based Tunkaseño students reported a larger perceived gap between their desired level of education and what level they believe to be possible than those living the United States, although the U.S. sample is small. As shown in Figure 2.5, Mexico-based students reported that they can complete, on average, 1.6 fewer years of schooling than they desire, while U.S.-based students reported only one year of difference. Nevertheless, due to sample size this difference is not statistically significant ($p - 0.5$). Importantly, over half of the Mexico-based students indicated no difference between their desired

55

level of education and what they believe to be feasible (51.4 percent). However, one-third of respondents (33.3 percent) reported a four to five-year educational aspiration/attainment gap. This period of time likely represents a college education.

Figure 2.5: The Tunkaseño Educational Aspiration/Attainment Gap, by Place of Residence

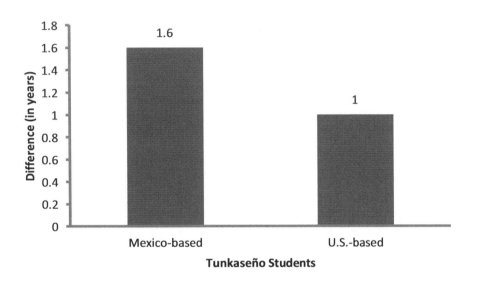

A Closer Look at Young Tunkaseños based in Yucatán

Given the observed variation in levels of schooling by age cohort, we chose to focus the rest of our analysis on interviewees who fall into the two youngest age cohorts: 15-25 years old and 26-35 years old. By examining those who are between 15 and 35 years old, we gain a more accurate understanding of the factors influencing current educational attainment in Tunkás. At the same time, in order to explore the effects of parental migration, we restricted our analysis to 15-35-year-olds living in Tunkás, thus excluding California-based interviewees. Figure 2.6 offers a demographic profile of these individuals, compared to broader segments of our sample.

We now explore the influence of school and teacher quality, parental involvement, and migration among Tunkaseños in our subgroup of interest. These interviewees had an average age of 24, and most of them were female. In terms of education, they averaged 10.8 years of schooling, or less than a high school education. Only 43.5 percent had completed high school or a vocational training program. Nevertheless, this percentage may increase with time, as almost a third of interviewees were still studying.

Figure 2.6: Demographic Profile of Tunkaseño Interviewees

Selected Demographic Characteristics	Tunkás-based interviewees aged 15-35 (n=198)	All Tunkás-based interviewees (n=490)	All Tunkaseños interviewed in Yucatán and U.S. (n=552)
Average age	23.9	39.4	39.6
Gender	38.7% male 61.3% female	39.7% male 60.3% female	41.9% male 58.1% female
Average years of education	10.8 years	9.0 years	9.1 years
Percentage of high school graduates	43.5[27]	26.1	26.3
Percentage still studying	32.8	15.5	15.4

Perceptions of School Quality in Tunkás

We asked our respondents to rate various aspects of school quality, with reference to the last school they attended. Specifically, we asked about facilities, curriculum, teacher ability, regularity of classes, and student safety. Evidence from our standardized survey as well as our qualitative interviews paints a mixed portrait of school quality in Tunkás. As shown in Figure 2.7, more than three-quarters of interviewees aged 15-35 living in Tunkás had a positive opinion of the town's school facilities.

---

[27]This figure is calculated from a sample that excludes current students (n=115). The overall high school completion rate for all 15-35-year-olds living in Tunkás is 36.0 percent (n=172).

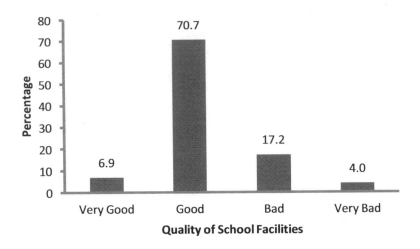

However, our in-depth interviews with Tunkaseño parents, educators and students do not reflect the evaluation captured by our standardized survey. María Luisa explained that some of the classrooms in her son's high school "used to be [animal] pens. They only put up some rods to keep animals out. There is no air conditioning, no fans. It's not worthy of being a school." Similarly, Francisco, a high school teacher, told us:

> The school where I teach used to be a shelter donated by the *ejidatarios*. They remodeled the windows and doors because there were none in the classrooms. The courtyards were destroyed when they came to do the remodeling, and they did not repair them.

At another school, a teacher expressed concern over rotting windows and doors and an outdated electrical system. Although she has put in a request for assistance from the government, she explained that there is a long list of requests from other schools. We believe that our survey interviewees may have rated their school facilities as "good" because they are comparing them to the past conditions of these structures. In sum, while the town's school facilities have improved, there remains much work to be done.

Perceptions of Teacher Quality in Tunkás

Generally, students residing in Tunkás had positive perceptions of teacher quality; 72.5 percent described their teachers as "good," and another 15.6 percent described them as "very good." In Tunkás a teacher's role is not isolated to his/her classroom. We learned that quite often the teacher must take on additional responsibilities in the school. In one school the teacher also serves as the principal. At another school the teachers help with the cleaning of the school because they do not have a janitorial staff. With these added responsibilities, teachers in Tunkás have expanded influence over the lives of their students. Consequently, we wanted to explore how their work was perceived by their students and the impact that it may have on their educational attainment.

Looking specifically at one area of teacher quality, we asked respondents about their teachers' expectations for them, either currently or when they attended school. We read a series of four statements about teacher expectations and asked interviewees to state their level of agreement with each of those statements.[28] We then created a summative index to measure interviewees' overall impressions of teacher expectations.[29] The higher the respondent's score on this index, the higher the perceived teacher expectations. As shown in Figure 2.8, we found that the average level of perceived teacher expectations among Tunkás-based interviewees aged 15-35 was 9.4 on a 12-point scale.

Figure 2.8. Perceived Teacher Expectations among Interviewees Aged 15-35 in Tunkás

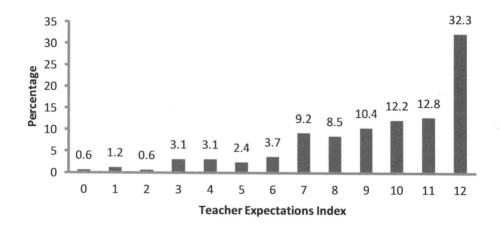

---

[28]The statements were: "My teachers are/were in interested in my school work", "My teachers expect/expected me to finish high school", "My teachers talk/talked to me frequently about attending a university", and "My teachers expect/expected me to finish a college degree."

[29]For each question, the individual's response was numerically coded from 0 to 3. 0 corresponded to "strongly disagree" and 3 to "strongly agree." Consequently, the score on the teacher index could range from 0 to 12.

Almost one-third of Tunkaseños in the age cohort of interest strongly agreed that their teachers demonstrated interest in them and had high expectations for them. Over half of this group (57.3 percent) had scores of 10, 11 or 12—the highest levels of teacher expectations.

To determine if high teacher expectations are associated with higher levels of educational attainment, we compared the average scores on the teacher index of high school graduates with those who had not finished high school.[30] We found that Tunkás-based high school graduates between the ages of 15-35 had an average teacher expectation score of 10.1, while non-high school graduates had a score of 8.7. This difference is statically significant (p=.01), suggesting that higher teacher expectations may positively influence educational attainment.

Tunkaseños whom we interviewed in depth echoed the importance of their teachers' expectations for their educational attainment. For example, Lisa recalled how her teachers would encourage her to get good grades in order to attend a university—which she currently does. Federico, a current high school student, provided a more mixed picture of teacher expectations:

> The majority of my teachers are very nice people, and they give you advice. They encourage you to finish your studies. But there are others who don't. We do not pay attention to them; we only listen to teachers who encourage us.

In sum, evidence from both qualitative interviews and survey data gathered in Tunkás provide support for the idea that a positive relationship exists between teacher quality, specifically a teacher's expectations, and a student's educational attainment. However, multivariate analysis is needed to confirm that this relationship holds when accounting for other variables.

Effects of Parental Education and Involvement

The influence of parents on their children's educational attainment has been extensively documented in previous research. Among our survey interviewees in Tunkás, the average level of father and mother's education was 4.2 years and 4.4 years of schooling, respectively. For those in our subgroup of principal interest (currently living in

---

[30]Current students are excluded from any analysis in this chapter that compares high school graduates with non-high school graduates.

Tunkás and aged 15-35), the average level of a father's education was 5.5 years and 6.4 years for the mother.

Consistent with our analysis of teacher quality, we wanted to explore if parent education was related to high school completion. In order to see if there was a statistically significant relationship between parental educational attainment and a child's education, we compared the average years of mother's schooling among high school graduates with that of interviewees who did not graduate from high school. Among high school graduates aged 15-35 and living in Tunkás, their mothers had an average of 7.1 years of schooling. Among those in the same cohort who did not finish high school, their mothers had 3.9 years of schooling. This difference is highly significant statistically ($p=.00$), suggesting that a mother's education is positively associated with her child's educational attainment. Again, multivariate analysis is necessary to determine if this finding holds when accounting for other factors.[31]

The second type of parental influence that we explored was parents' personal involvement in their children's education. We asked current and past students if their parents had participated in a list of five activities: speaking with them about their homework, discussing higher education, asking about their grades, talking with their teachers, and attending school events. Figure 2.9 shows the percentage of Tunkás-based interviewees aged 15-35 who reported that their parents had participated in each of these activities.

---

[31]We performed the same analysis focusing on the influence of the father's education, with similar results. The average years of father's schooling among high school graduates aged 15-35 and living in Tunkás was 6.4, compared with 3.6 years of schooling among those who did not finish high school. This difference is statically significant ($p=.00$), suggesting that a father's education does have a positive relationship with his child's high school completion.

Figure 2.9: Reported Parental Involvement in Children's Education

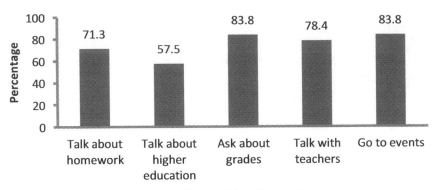

Young Tunkaseños report high levels of parental involvement in their academic lives. More than eight in ten indicated that their parents asked about their grades and had gone to school events. Over 70 percent said that their parents had talked to them about homework and had discussed their child's progress with their teachers. The least frequent activity reported by our respondents was talking about higher education with their parents. Over 40 percent indicated their parents had never talked to them about pursuing higher education.

We created a summative index of parental involvement. For every activity in which a parent participated, he/she received one point on the index. Accordingly, the highest possible value is five and the lowest possible value is zero. Among all respondents, their average score on the parental involvement index was 3.2, with a slightly higher score of 3.7 among our subgroup of interest (aged 15-35, living in Tunkás). Among interviewees who had completed high school, the average level of parental involvement was 4.0, compared with 3.2 among non-high school graduates. This difference is statistically significant (p=.01), suggesting a positive relationship between parental involvement and high school completion. Coupled with our findings on the relationship between parents' educational level and the educational attainment of their children, we find preliminary support that parents do have a significant influence on their child's education, subject to confirmation through multivariate analysis.

Absent Parents and Educational Attainment

Although Tunkás is a high-emigration town, just a small fraction of Tunkás-based interviewees aged 15-35 reported currently having at least one parent who lives in the United States (5.3 percent). At the same time, 17.2 percent of young people living in Tunkás indicated that either one or both of their parents were living in another part of Mexico. In other words, one in five (20.7 percent) Tunkás-based youth had at least one international or internal migrant parent.

Those who currently have a migrant parent averaged 11.3 years of schooling, while those whose parents were living in Tunkás averaged 10.7 years of schooling, a difference that is not statistically significant. However, this measure does not perfectly capture the influence of parental migration on a child's educational attainment because of the cross-sectional nature of our study. It is possible that at another point in time a young Tunkaseño *did* have a parent living in the United States and that their absence did affect his/her educational attainment. It is also possible that a person who currently has a parent living abroad had both parents present in Tunkás during his/her period of schooling.

Since previous research has demonstrated that the negative effects of parental migration on educational attainment may be mitigated by a migrant parent's financial contributions, we also explored the effects of remittances. Roughly one-quarter of young people in Tunkás were living in a household that was receiving remittances at the time of our survey. Of those whose families were receiving remittances, one-third reported that they were using a portion of these funds for school expenses. Interviewees aged 15-35 in remittance-receiving households averaged 11.3 years of schooling, compared with 10.6 years among those living in households that were not receiving remittances – a statistically insignificant difference in educational achievement.

We also explored whether migrant remittances influence high-school completion rates. After excluding current students, we found that 54.2 percent of interviewees in remittance-receiving families had graduated from high school, compared with a 40.7 percent graduation rate among who did not currently having a migrant parent. Again, we do not find a statistically significant difference between the two groups. Nevertheless, looking at a family's financial situation at a specific point in time may not provide us with reliable information about the influence of remittances on a young person's educational attainment (see Sawyer, 2014).

Our qualitative interviews shed light on why simply receiving remittances may not translate into increased educational attainment. A common theme that surfaced in these interviews was the lack of "administrative" skills that some Tunkáseño women display in using remittance income. Gloria, a Tunkaseña in her twenties, provided us with the example of a neighbor:

> Around the corner lives a woman whose husband migrated when their son was two years old. The son is now 16 years old. With the money that the mother has received all of these years, she bought some property and built her house. But she never finished the construction of her home, and she has no money left. She takes out loans from the bank and spends it on entertaining herself and her friends in Izamál [a nearby city].

Gloria further explained that not all women misuse remittances; it depends on "the education and personal values of the person responsible for the funds." This suggests that it is not simply the sending and receiving of remittances that may influence the educational attainment of a child; proper administration of the funds is also essential.[32]

A MULTIVARIATE ANALYSIS OF EDUCATIONAL ATTAINMENT

Modeling Years of Schooling

While bivariate analysis suggested a significant influence of parents and teachers on a young Tunkaseño's educational attainment, we conducted a multivariate regression analysis to see if the relationship still holds when accounting for other factors. Educational attainment, our dependent variable, is operationalized as the total number of school years completed. The independent variables in the model measure these predictors of educational attainment: involvement of parents in their children's education, teacher quality, and parents' migration. With regard to the influence of parents, we included a measure of the mother's level of education[33] and the summative index of parental involvement described above. To measure the influence of teachers, we used our

---

[32]Similarly, Sawyer (2013) found that remittances by themselves cannot increase educational attainment. His case studies of remittance-receiving youth in rural Mexico highlight the influence of the direct remittance recipient (i.e., the mother).

[33] We replicated the model with father's level of education and there were no significant changes to our findings.

summative index of teacher expectations. The influence of migration is measured by whether an interviewee had at least one parent living outside of Tunkás and whether the household was receiving remittances. Because of the inclusion of these migration variables, we restricted the analysis to respondents living in Tunkás at the time of our fieldwork.

Table 2.1 presents the results of our multivariate analysis of the educational attainment of Tunkás-based interviewees aged 15-35. We find that educational attainment is significantly and positively influenced by the mother's level of education (p=.028), the expectations of teachers (p=.050), and household wealth (p=.007). While previous research has emphasized that educational attainment is best predicted by individual and family characteristics, versus school and teacher characteristics, our analysis suggests that in the case of Tunkaseño youth, both types of factors play a role in explaining attainment.

Migration-related variables do not significantly predict educational attainment among Tunkaseño youth. However, as in our bivariate analysis, caution must be taken in interpreting these results, given the cross-sectional nature of our study. It could be that a parent was in fact outside of Tunkás at some point during a respondent's education but now lives in Tunkás. It also could be true that a family received remittances in prior years that helped with schooling. Consequently, these variables may not adequately capture the influence of migration on schooling.

Table 2.1: Multivariate Analysis of Educational Attainment
(coefficient estimates; standard errors in parentheses)

Mother's Education	**.163**</br>(.074)**
Parent Involvement Index	.051</br>(.189)
Teacher Expectations Index	**.192**</br>(.097)**
Current Migrant Parent	.008</br>(.593)
Remittance Receiving Household	-.092</br>(.593)
Prospera Participant	-.276</br>(.512)
Male	.279</br>(.538)
Age	-.034</br>(.043)
Household Wealth	**.281***</br>(.102)**
Constant	**7.169***</br>(1.637)**
N	129
R^2	.258
Adjusted R^2	.201

***significant at .01 level.   **significant at .05 level.   *significant at .10 level.

Table 2.2: Logit Analysis of High School Completion or the Equivalent
(coefficient estimates; standard errors in parentheses)

Mother's Education	**.164**** **(.081)**
Parent Involvement Index	-.072 (.199)
Teacher Expectations Index	.152 (.111)
Current Migrant Parent	.089 (.697)
Remittance Receiving Household	-.893 (.717)
Prospera Participant	.550 (.565)
Male	-.023 (.629)
Age	**-.147***** **(.057)**
Household Wealth	**.294**** **(.126)**
Constant	-.162 (1.921)
N	88

***significant at .01 level.   **significant at .05 level.   *significant at .10 level.

As in our first model, we find no statistically significant relationship between our migration variables and high school completion. Additionally, while teacher expectations were significantly related to overall years of schooling in our first model, in our second model we do not find this variable to be a significant predictor of high school completion. However, we find that parental education, age, and household wealth are all associated with high school completion. Tunkaseños in our sample whose mothers had higher levels of education, were younger, and had higher levels of household wealth were significantly more likely to have graduated from high school.[34]

Despite its significance in our bivariate analysis, parental involvement was not found to be a significant predictor of overall educational attainment nor high school completion in particular. Nevertheless, our qualitative interviews with Tunkaseños on both sides of the border provide support that parents' actions do play a vital role in their children's education, with many students reporting that their parents are quite active in their academic life. For example, many of our interviewees described parents' desire and verbal encouragement for their children to continue their education even in the face of severe economic constraints. José, a current student, explained how his parents, especially his mother, voiced a strong desire for him to finish his schooling: "My mom always supported us to keep studying, because it's necessary. She grew up on a farm and never went to school, but she gave us schooling." Similarly, many interviewees reported that their parents want their children to advance academically in ways that the parents were not able to do. Such testimony helps to explain the link between parental education and educational attainment. If parents are expressing a desire for their children to complete more schooling than they did, children whose parents possess higher levels of education would potentially complete more schooling than those whose parents have fewer years of studies.

Students with whom we spoke on both sides of the border also point to their parents as a motivator to stay in school. They told us that they want to complete their education, enabling them to give back to their parents. Alejandra, a current student in Tunkás, explained:

---

[34]Sawyer (2014) has reported similar results. He found that maternal education levels and household wealth were the variables most associated with parental aspirations and educational attainment in a rural Mexican community.

> My parents constantly tell me that I need to finish school because they
> have worked hard and that their goal is that I finish school. It's also a
> goal of mine, because they have struggled for many years so that I
> could study and if I don't finish, it'd be a big disappointment for them.

This sentiment also was expressed by Tunkaseños living in the United States who view their parents' migration as a sacrifice to provide them with better academic opportunities. When asked what motivated him to go to school, Santos, a freshman in college, answered: "My family is everything to me. I just want to give everything back to them. They are the reason why I'm going to college. I want to get a better life for all of us." Santos' words show how students view their education as a form of repayment to their parents, benefiting everyone in the family.

Through our in-depth interviews we also learned how the adult school is making a difference in the lives of Tunkaseño parents and their children. Some parents reported that they returned to adult school in order to lead their children by example. Esther, a mother attending the adult school, explained why she continued her education, "More than anything, I want to set an example for my children that it is never too late to continue [with your education]." Moreover, parents who attend the adult school feel that there is a new dynamic between themselves and their children: They can support each other in their educational pursuits. When asked about the role that adult education plays in her relationship with her daughter, Elena, a mother who attends the adult school explained: "Some of things in the homework are new to me, and sometimes I don't understand it. I ask my daughter and if she doesn't understand something in her homework she asks for my help. We exchange information." Esther, the mother mentioned above who also attends the adult school, echoed this dynamic:

> I'm one year ahead of my son, so I can help him in his homework.
> That's something that I couldn't do before, because I didn't have any
> idea what he was studying. Now when he has homework, he asks me
> for help.

This type of relationship, in which parents and children help each other with homework, may not be common at higher grade levels. Lisa, the college student mentioned previously, reported that although her parents were very active in encouraging her academic pursuits, they often could not help her with her schoolwork because they did not understand it. This is not surprising, given that the average education level of parents of 15-35 year olds in Tunkás is less than completed primary school. Parents with higher levels of education may be able to help their children in their studies in different ways, which lead their children to be able to complete higher levels of education.

OBSTACLES TO EDUCATIONAL ATTAINMENT

While the above models provide valuable information about the factors that influence educational attainment among young Tunkaseños, they only tell part of the story. Through survey and qualitative interviewing, we gained a deeper understanding of the constraints on Tunkaseños as they pursue an education. We asked our interviewees to identify the obstacles that a young person faces when trying to finish high school in Mexico. Figure 2.10 shows the obstacles most frequently reported by Tunkás interviewees in our key age range (15-35 years).

Figure 2.10: Perceived Obstacles to Completing High School in Mexico

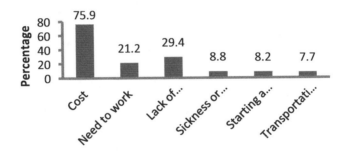

Most Frequently Reported Obstacles to Finishing High School

Economic obstacles were by far the most frequently cited. Over 70 percent of respondents noted cost as an obstacle to finishing their high school education, while around 20 percent mentioned the related need to work. When we asked respondents to select the most important obstacle to high school completion, among those they had mentioned, 60 percent responded that cost was the principal obstacle.

To ease the financial burden of education, some families participate in Prospera, a federal government program previously known as Oportunidades. This program provides monetary scholarships to families living in poverty to assist with the cost of food, health, and education (Coordinación Nacional de Prospera Programa de Inclusion Social 2014a, 2014b). If a family is eligible for Prospera, it receives scholarships for each child, the amount varying by grade level and gender. In order to receive this aid there are

70

attendance requirements for the child, and the family must attend community workshops. It is important to note, however, that the financial assistance does not necessarily cover all of a family's educational expenses.

There is also a potential for misuse of Prospera funds, given limited supervision of how the mother is spending the money. While teachers reported that some Tunkaseño families do misuse the monetary assistance they receive through Prospera, the program continues to be important and necessary to reduce the economic burden that schooling puts on low-income families. When we asked Alma, an elementary school teacher, if she believed that removing Prospera would have an effect on her school, she responded: "It would have a negative effect because there are mothers who use that money to buy [school-required] uniforms and school supplies that they still need."

Only certain families meet the income qualifications for Prospera. Those who do not rely on other types of government support to defray the costs of educating their children, which in addition to school supplies and uniforms can include textbooks, special fees, and other expenses. Until the end of middle school, the government provides Tunkaseño children with items like shoes, backpacks, and even some school supplies. A mother of three described the importance of receiving this aid, noting that it was a principal reason for her family to migrate from the resort city of Cancún to Tunkás:

> We actually came to Tunkás for my son. I got sick. It was either my illness or his education. I started receiving treatment and we didn't have money to enroll him. In Cancún, enrollment costs 1,800 pesos for high school. Here [in Tunkás] there's a lot of government support. In Cancún the only thing they give the elementary children is a backpack.

While government assistance for educational costs in Tunkás is greater at the elementary and middle school levels, it dwindles in high school. Although high school students receive a laptop which they can keep upon graduation, the cost of supplies, textbooks, and school fees fall completely on the families. It is important to note that while most people in Tunkás complete their middle school education, most dropouts occur during high school. Less government support for high school students could be a factor in these dropouts.

Although fewer than one in ten in our survey mentioned romantic relationships and starting a family as obstacles to completing high school, when we spoke to those who left school before completing a given level (elementary, middle, high school. or college) 17.7 percent reported that they dropped out because they were starting a family. This

71

theme also emerged frequently in our in-depth interviews. When we asked about the common challenges that young people in Tunkás face when it comes to their education, numerous interviewees said that young people leave school due to romantic relationships. They specifically mentioned the pregnancy of a young girl as the reason she and her boyfriend do not complete their studies. Lisa, the university student quoted above, identified teen pregnancy as the most common reason students in Tunkás abandon their schooling:

> What I've seen is that a lot of young men have girlfriends and stop studying in order to support their girlfriend if she gets pregnant. When I was studying in Tunkás ten years ago, it was: school, home, school, home. That's how it was because my friends were like that too. But now, the young girls only think about having boyfriends, boyfriends, boyfriends.

Lisa's comments suggest another general theme that surfaced frequently in our interviews: a lack of interest in education. Some respondents reported that the only reason some young men attend school is to see their girlfriends; they have no interest in their schoolwork. About one in three survey respondents indicated that lack of interest is an obstacle to finishing high school (see Figure 2.10, above).

Alcohol and drug use was also mentioned frequently in our qualitative interviews with teachers, parents and students. While fewer than one in ten survey respondents cited substance abuse as an obstacle for completing high school, much previous research has found that substance abuse is highly correlated with poor academic outcomes. Our qualitative interviews revealed that this problem is a new and growing concern in the community. A middle school parent described the recent steps local teachers have taken to address the issue: "The teachers called a meeting with all the parents because they wanted to inform us that the drugs are circulating around the school. They were trying to figure out who the dealers are, in order to take further actions." In the following section we explore this newly emergent concern in greater detail.

IMPACTS OF ALCOHOL AND DRUG USE ON EDUCATIONAL ATTAINMENT

Previous research on alcohol and substance use in Mexico provides insights into consumption patterns of different age groups over time. The most recent National Survey of Addiction, conducted by the Instituto Nacional de Salud Pública (INSP), found a significant increase in alcohol consumption among Mexicans aged 18-65 and 12-17, compared to consumption rates in 2008.[35] Additionally, the percentage of Mexicans who began drinking before age 17 increased from 49 percent in 2008 to 55 percent in 2011 (INSP, 2011). The INSP found that although men generally consume alcohol in greater proportions than women, there is a smaller gender gap in the youngest age cohort. Among those 12-17 years old, 17 percent of males and 11 percent of females reported consuming alcohol at high rates, compared to 47 percent of males and 20 percent of females in the 18-34 age group (INSP, 2011). Thus, adolescents in Mexico are now consuming alcohol at similar rates, regardless of gender.

With regard to drug use, the INSP (2011) reported that marijuana and cocaine were the most common drugs consumed in Mexico, respectively. Despite the abovementioned decreasing gender gap in alcohol consumption, a large gap still exists for drug use. Men had the highest rates of drug consumption: an average of 4.2 males reported drug use for every 1 woman who reported such use. The INSP survey found that males who had been exposed to drugs by family or friends, who were not in school, and who perceived drug use as low-risk were the most likely to consume drugs at least once in their lives. Mexicans begin using drugs at an older age than alcohol, with an average of 20.1 years for women and 18.3 years for men (INSP, 2011). The 18-34-year group had the highest rate of drug use, pointing to a recent introduction of drugs and the development of a drug culture in some parts of Mexico.

Numerous studies have found a strong correlation between alcohol and drug abuse among adolescents and poor academic performance (see, for example, Chakravarthy, Shah & Lotifpour, 2013). This poor school performance could be a result of learning difficulties caused early alcohol and drug consumption (Gutierrez & Sher, 2015: 208), or it may reflect poor school attendance related to substance abuse (Greenblatt 2000). In addition to lower grades and increased truancy, students who use alcohol and drugs are more likely to drop out of school than those who do not. The National Center on Addiction and Substance Abuse at Columbia University (2001: 3) found that high schoolers who frequently used alcohol and drugs were up to five times

---

[35]INSP (2011) found that in 2008 among those ages 18 to 65, 67.9 percent reported ever consuming alcohol compared to 77.1 percent in 2011. A similar increase was noted for those ages 12 to 17, 31.7 percent in 2008 and 42.9 percent in 2011 reported ever consuming alcohol.

more likely to drop out of high school compared to their peers. The relationship between substance use and poor educational outcomes is especially worrisome because, if adolescents are not going to school, they are also not gaining crucial skills needed to enter the workforce and achieve social mobility. This underdevelopment of human capital perpetuates an even greater cycle of alcohol and substance abuse (Aguila, Mejia, Perez-Arce, Ramirez & Rivera, 2015). Thus it is important to identify risk factors and enhance protective factors relating to substance abuse.

Parental Migration as a Risk Factor for Alcohol and Drug Use

Earlier in this chapter we discussed the conflicting effects of migration on educational attainment. But to gain a fuller understanding of how migration affects adolescents' school performance, it is important to explore the ways it affects young people *outside* of the classroom, especially in terms of risk behaviors like alcohol and drug use.

Previous research has identified a positive association between having an absent parent and an increased probability of adolescent alcohol use. Adolescents with at least one such parent consume alcohol at higher levels than those living with both parents. Moreover, adolescents with both an absent parent(s) and a history of parental alcoholism have an even higher probability of alcohol lifetime dependency (Thompson, 2008). An increased likelihood to engage in such behavior could be explained by changes in family dynamics resulting from having the head of the family absent for an indefinite period of time, the creation of additional stressors for wives and children, and a mother's diminished ability to monitor and control her child's behaviors without the help of the father (Borges, et al., 2007). Other research, however, has identified protective factors that mitigate the influence of a migrant parent. For example, Lippold et al. (2014) have suggested that while an adolescent's surroundings (e.g., a household with a parent who has migrated) do influence the likelihood of a child to engage in problem behaviors like substance use, the mother's involvement may help alleviate some of these negative effects. They found that active parental monitoring efforts have significant effects on delinquency and substance abuse. Monitoring a child's behavior, the mother's knowledge of the child's activities, and a good relationship between mother and child were all found to have mediating effects on adolescent substance use. It follows that while the absence of a parent due to migration may lead to less control or supervision of an adolescent, the relationship between the non-migrant parent and the adolescent is important in determining whether a child initiates drug use.

Alcohol and Drug Use in Tunkás

Through our survey we were able to gain a broad understanding of alcohol and drug activity among adolescents in Tunkás. We asked participants to tell us the frequency of alcohol and drug use during a variety of situations.[36] Figure 2.11 shows perceptions of alcohol use in the community. As can be seen, the majority of respondents (over 70 percent) indicated that alcohol is consumed most frequently at the town fiestas, dances, concerts and other music events. Additionally, roughly half of respondents indicated that young people sometimes drink at home when they are unsupervised (48.0 percent), at baseball or soccer games (50.4 percent), after school with their classmates (44.9 percent,) and on the weekends or days off from school (53.8 percent).

Figure 2.11: Location and Frequency of Adolescent Alcohol Use in Tunkás

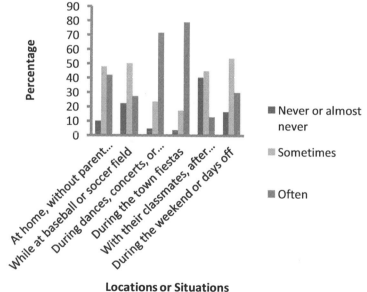

<hr />

[36]Respondents could categorize the frequency as "very often," "sometimes," or "never or almost never."

While drug consumption is not as prevalent, it is slowly becoming more common in Tunkás. Figure 2.12 shows that drug use largely mirrors alcohol consumption patterns in terms of location. Again, respondents indicated that adolescents used drugs most frequently at the town fiestas (48.8 percent), dances, concerts, and other music events (48.2 percent).

Figure 2.12: Location and Frequency of Adolescent Drug Use in Tunkás

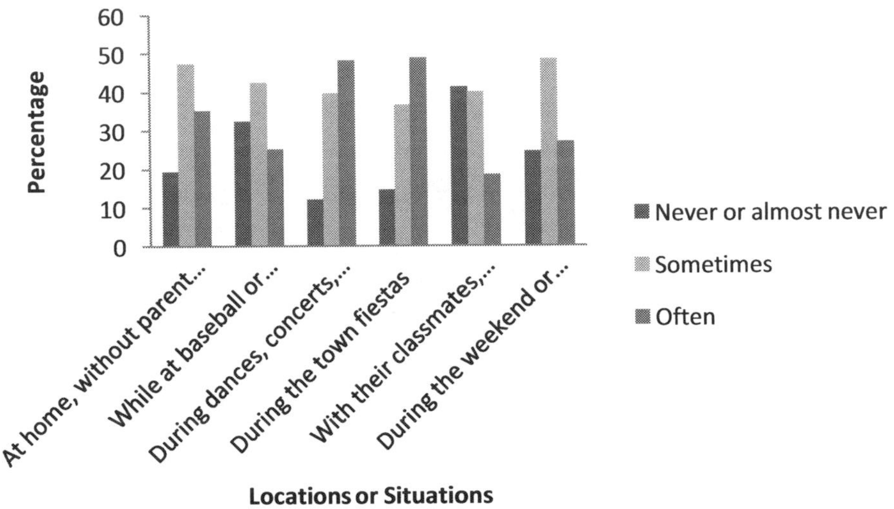

Access and Exposure to Alcohol and Drugs in Tunkás

Our in-depth interviews revealed a growing normalization of alcohol use in Tunkás. Many of our interviewees expressed the belief that because alcohol consumption is seen as normal or natural, sometimes family members provide alcohol to minors. However, our survey data do not support this claim. Only 7.3 percent of respondents reported that young people are given alcohol by a family member. Figure 2.13 presents further information on perceptions of alcohol access in Tunkás for respondents between 15-25 years of age.[37]

---

[37]We focus here on those aged 15-25 since they presumably have more accurate knowledge about where adolescents are accessing alcohol and drugs.

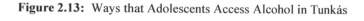

Figure 2.13: Ways that Adolescents Access Alcohol in Tunkás

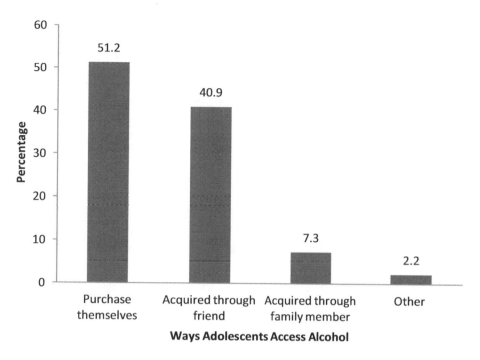

We found that over half (51.2 percent) of interviewees between the ages of 15-25 said that adolescents purchase alcohol for themselves, and 40.9 percent believed that adolescents access alcohol through friends.[38] Our qualitative interviews revealed more about how young people are able to purchase alcohol, despite the legal prohibition on selling alcohol to minors. Numerous interviewees told how easy it is for minors to obtain alcohol through *clandestinos*, illegal businesses that are accessible 24 hours a day, 7 days a week. Julio, a 21-year-old taxi driver, described how the *clandestinos* work:

> *Clandestinos* operate the entire day. As a taxi driver, when I am asked to go to a location, I have to take them regardless of my knowledge of the place. When people leave the *clandestino* they come back to my taxi and I am able to see that they have purchased alcohol. Sometimes even the bartenders [in licensed bars] will sell alcohol to minors.

---

[38]Percentages do not sum to 100.0 because interviewees could choose more than one method of accessing alcohol and drugs.

Once a minor is able to locate a *clandestino*, he then mentions it to his friends. Despite widespread awareness of *clandestinos* among the town's residents, our interviewees reported that only limited efforts have been made to shut down these illegal operations.

We also asked our survey respondents about where young Tunkaseños are accessing drugs. As shown in Figure 2.14, among Tunkaseños aged 15-25, most believed that adolescents access drugs through friends or purchase the drugs themselves (57.7 percent and 52.2 percent, respectively). Our interviewees told us that there are a handful of known drug-dealers in the town. Despite this knowledge, residents are hesitant to speak about drug-related issues to local authorities because they run the risk of being harassed by *narcos* for intervening in the drug dealing process.

Figure 2.14: Ways Adolescents Access Drugs in Tunkás

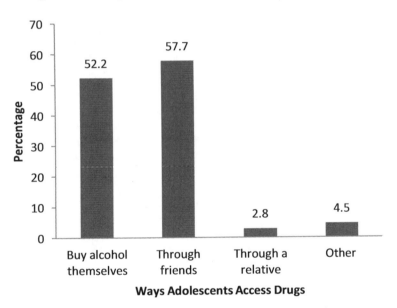

Our interviewees observed that while drugs are used less commonly than alcohol in Tunkás, they have become more prevalent during the last decade. About a decade ago, they reported, outsiders—people from other parts of the Yucatán Peninsula or the United States—introduced drugs such as amphetamines and narcotics to Tunkás. These outsiders came to the town posing as businessmen in order to recruit people to sell the drugs. Gloria, the 25-year-old married female quoted above, recalled being about 16 years old when drugs came to Tunkás. She explained how easy it is for drug dealers to recruit other dealers and to insert drugs further into the community:

> The dealers will ask potential dealers, 'Do you want to make easy money?' Once the person agrees, they discuss specifics and a relationship is established. Eventually, word gets around the town about who to obtain drugs from.

While drugs have only been available in Tunkás within the past decade, some interviewees predicted that, just as alcohol consumption has been normalized, smoking marijuana or doing other drugs will soon be considered natural as well.

Our qualitative interviews also provided evidence of a gendered aspect of access to alcohol and drugs in Tunkás. The majority of our interviewees identified a male—either a friend or a boyfriend—as the main source through which females are introduced to illicit substances. Gloria recalled how, as a young adolescent, she was introduced to marijuana through her then-boyfriend:

> My own husband, who was my boyfriend at the time, is the one who offered me [marijuana]. He asked me, 'You want some?' and I answered, 'Yes, I will have some. I don't want to be ignorant anymore and I'm curious about what the effects will be.

In addition to affecting the women in their lives, men involved with alcohol and drugs also influence other males in their peer groups. Respondents highlighted the notion of "*amigos, entre hombres*" as a key source of a culture of risk use among males. César, a 19-year-old Tunkaseño who was left in the care of his mother when his father migrated to the United States, first used marijuana at a friend's house. César mentioned that most men will use drugs as a social statement, to prove that they are braver or riskier than the other men around town.

We also found evidence of gendered drug consumption patterns among Tunkaseño adolescents. While there was a general consensus that both adolescent men and women engage in drinking and drug use, a majority of our interviewees pointed to a larger problem of addiction in the male population. Interestingly, they identified the gender of a young person's primary caretaker as one of the factors that differentiates consumption patterns of males and females. In cases where the mother is left as the sole caretaker of her children, boys are more likely than girls to partake in risk behaviors. Yesenia, a 48-year-old mother, explained: "A single mother will have an extremely challenging time raising her children, especially any boys. It is difficult to control them and get them to listen to the mother's rules."

A common theme that surfaced in our qualitative interviews was that a parent or guardian can serve as either a protective factor against or a risk factor for adolescents' consumption of alcohol and drugs. Consistent with prior research (Thompson, 2008), our respondents identified parental supervision as a positive influence for adolescents, especially boys, to avoid risk behaviors like alcoholism and drug addiction. On the other hand, a lack of supervision proved to be a risk factor. The topic of *demasiada libertad* -- excessive freedom and not enough supervision – came up many times in our interviews. Julio, the taxi driver quoted above, is a returned internal migrant who now stays in Tunkás to be closer to his parents. He explained the importance of his parents in keeping him on the right track:

> My parents limited my freedom, and thanks to that, I haven't taken the wrong path. I have former classmates who are now alcoholics. Their parents stopped being strict with them. Right now there are a lot of young males, 12 or 15 years old, who spend most their time drinking.

Marina, a mother of four, expressed the same concern: "There is too much freedom nowadays. Too many parents aren't aware of their children's whereabouts. This isn't right, because too many children are becoming drug addicts."

Another factor identified by our interviewees as predictive of adolescents' consumption of alcohol and drugs was the education they received at home. Interviewees cited "good morals" and "setting a good example" as key to keeping adolescents from engaging in alcohol and substance use. Marina explained: "One needs to educate their children, because in the end if they see you drinking, your children will be more likely to do it."

Effects of Migration on Adolescent Alcohol and Drug Consumption

Among our survey respondents who had at least one international migration experience, 42.5 percent reported leaving a child behind in Mexico on their most recent trip to the United States. Of these migrating parents, more than nine out of ten (91.8 percent) were men who had left their children behind with the mother of the child. We found no instances of a mother who had left her child in the care of the father on her most recent trip north. While there is no empirical evidence showing decreased parental ability to discipline children of the opposite sex, our qualitative interviews suggest that young boys feel greater agency to use alcohol and drugs when the mother is their caretaker and the father is absent due to migration.

Another explanation could be that a mother's authority is weakened when the migrant father retains power over the household. Gloria explained that if an absent father sends remittances he remains in charge of household's decisions, putting the caregiver in a secondary position:

> Young girls and boys will get grumpy and upset over any little thing and demand that their caregiver call their father to see what his opinion on the matter is. Since the father provides income to the family, in this town they have the mentality that he has the right to decide whether or not his child can get permission to go out.

This kind of situation creates a power dynamic within the family unit that adolescents internalize. While the adolescent may still respect their guardian, he/she will rapidly come to understand where the guardian stands in the hierarchy of power, allowing the child to manipulate the situation to obtain what they desire. On some occasions, a teenager will complain directly to the father about his/her caregiver. Gloria provided an example:

> Cristina complains to her father, "You know what dad, grandmother doesn't want to take me out on her trips to Izamal, and I really want to go with her." Then the father will order [the grandmother] to take his daughter on every trip to Izamal, so that the daughter can enjoy herself for a while.

Our survey data provide further evidence of how the absence of a migrant parent can be a risk factor in adolescent alcohol and drug consumption. We listed a variety of feelings and situations that a child with a migrant parent might experience. Respondents were asked to specify which of these feelings or situations applied to a child with a parent absent due to migration.

As shown in Figure 2.15, a majority of respondents believed that a child with a migrant parent feels abandoned (82.8 percent), different from others (81.2 percent), and neglected (67.9 percent). Armando, a returned migrant who has experienced drug culture in the United States and Mexico, made the connection between negative feelings stemming from the absence of a parent and an increased risk of alcoholism and drug addiction. Referring to adolescents left behind, he said, "If they are left behind feeling down and feeling abandoned, they might think that there is nothing left to do than drink alcohol." Thus, negative feelings like abandonment, combined with the limited supervision that possibly results from a parent's absence, can increase the risk of adolescent alcohol and substance use.

Figure 2.15: Perceived Effects of an Absent Parent on Tunkaseño Adolescents

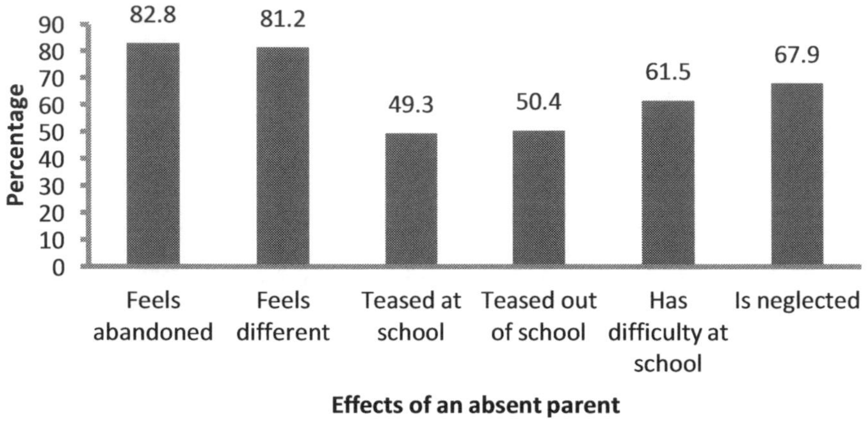

We also asked our survey interviewees about the experiences of the child of a migrant parent in relation to school and interactions with his/her peers. As can be seen in Figure 2.15, a majority (61.5 percent) of respondents believed that a child with a migrant parent struggles in school. Difficulties in school are not surprising, since feelings of abandonment, neglect, and "being different" that many children of migrants experience take a toll on their academic performance. Moreover, roughly half of our interviewees reported that a child with an absent parent gets teased by his/her peers, in and out of school (49.3 percent and 50.4 percent, respectively).

In our conversations with Tunkaseños about the impacts of parental migration on adolescent alcohol and drug use, many mentioned the role of remittances. In some cases, because adolescents have access to increased funds through remittances, they are able to purchase alcohol and drugs. For example, Gloria described a sister who sends remittances back home to her elderly parents and younger siblings. The siblings "are happy with their sister because when they go out, they always have money in their wallet and as a result can easily buy drugs or alcohol." In this case, migrant remittances increase an adolescent's disposable income that can be spent on drugs or alcohol.

But other Tunkaseños whom we interviewed took the position that that parental migration is not a significant risk factor for adolescent alcohol and drug use. They noted that, whether they have migrant parents or not, some adolescents engage in these risk behaviors. In fact, some Tunkaseños do not point to parental migration but rather the migration of the adolescents themselves as the primary risk factor for alcohol and drug use. Gloria provided an explanation for why this may be the case:

> Migrants who come from the United States, Cancún, and Playa del Carmen [another Yucatán resort city] bring consumption habits back. You know what really happens with adolescents? The mom and dad supervise adolescents here, so it is harder for them to consume, but over there they are independent and free to do as they wish, so they consume.

Thus, the lack of supervision that stems from a young person migrating away from his/her family serves to increase risk behaviors. Given their newfound freedom and independence, as well as greater disposable income, alcohol and drug consumption may seem like an easily accessible and possibly attractive activity for young migrants.

Returned migrants whom we interviewed also reported that drug-related habits come from their time outside of Tunkás. As Julio, a young returned migrant, explained:

> Drugs come from places like the United States and Cancún. That is where adolescents pick up the habit. In fact, there are a lot of people who return from Cancún and start offering drugs to others here.

Echoing Julio, César told the story of a friend who migrated to Cancún to work in a restaurant and was introduced to alcohol, cigarettes, and drugs:

> Before [migrating], he didn't drink or smoke. Now when you see him, he lights up a cigarette, and once it is done, he will light up another. He also drinks excessively, all kinds of alcohol.

Both men identified migration, to the United States or to cities like Cancún where substance abuse is more common than in Tunkás, as the way in which young people are most likely to pick up drug use. They then bring these risk behaviors back with them to their hometown.

83

Changes in Adolescent Behavior Resulting from Alcohol and Drug Use

Alcohol and drug use among Tunkaseño adolescents begins to permeate many aspects of their lives. For example, in their dress, young people begin to gravitate toward more non-traditional outfits that reflect their interest in drugs and alcohol. Gloria provided the example of her younger brother:

> My brother used to enjoy dressing like my husband, who has a western cowboy style. After exactly one week of visiting Mérida with an aunt, my brother no longer wore his boots. He began to purchase sneakers. He asked my mother to buy him a different style and size of clothing. For example, his shirts would no longer be fitted. They began to be enormous since he purchased the triple X size. The common theme that I began to observe in these kids was their desire to purchase hats and clothes that had the marijuana signature trade mark on them.

In addition to changes in dress, young Tunkaseños also evidence a change in attitude. Some interviewees, like Julio, noted that adolescents may become more aggressive under the influence of drugs or alcohol. He described how on one occasion, after he had been drinking, he confronted his parents:

> That experience is very painful for me to talk about, because the education that my parents instilled in me was not based on being disrespectful and using alcohol. Being disrespectful in that way was something that I learned from my friends. They were disrespectful toward their parents and I thought to myself, "Since they do it, why can't I?"

Julio's example highlights the potential negative influences of one's peer group, especially when alcohol or drugs are involved. As mentioned above, young Tunkaseño males often want to prove themselves among their friends, which can lead them not only to use alcohol and drugs but also to distance themselves from their parents and to develop a more aggressive attitude toward them.

Our interviewees agreed that alcohol and drug use influence the school-related behavior of Tunkaseño adolescents. Students' consumption of alcohol and drugs has become a growing concern in Tunkás' educational community, resulting in a series of meetings convened by teachers to work with parents on the issue. During these meetings it was reported that students sometimes skip school in order to drink or do drugs off-campus. It is not uncommon to see young Tunkaseños "with their bottles on the streets."

Marina described how the community works together to inform each other of any irregular behavior they witness among children:

> At any time throughout the day they sell alcohol in Tunkás. If a mother knows or believes her son went to school that morning because he left with his school stuff, but later is told in a parent meeting with the instructor that her son did not attend school that day, the mother will be in utter disbelief. But there will always be that other mom, who comes forward to the mother and says, "That day I saw your son drinking beer."

Marina's comment illustrates four important themes concerning adolescent alcohol and drug use in Tunkás. First, it points to the relatively easy access to alcohol and drugs for youth in Tunkás. Second, it highlights that youth do not feel worried about the potential consequences of being seen in public with alcohol, even though they are underage, which suggests the ineffectiveness of local authorities in dealing with the issue. Third, it shows the negative influence that substance abuse can have on a youth's academic performance. Finally, it suggests that the community is trying to find ways to combat this growing problem in Tunkás.

Previous research has noted the increased risk of drug consumption when an individual is not exposed to prevention programs, and the low number of individuals who get treated for dependency.[39] As rates of addiction have increased and may still be on the rise (especially among adolescents), there is great value in boosting investments in prevention and rehabilitation programs. Although alcohol and drug use is a growing concern in Tunkás, many of our interviewees noted that little has been done to prevent substance abuse. Some interviewees mentioned that local authorities have failed to enforce the laws. For example, we were told that if a police officer catches a youth using drugs, the officer may ask for money in exchange for not telling the parent. Figure 2.16 presents our survey data on community preferences for helping adolescents avoid alcohol and drug-related problems.

---

[39]For example, the INSP's most recent national survey of addiction found that just 6.8 percent of Mexicans who report alcohol dependency have received treatment (Instituto Nacional de Salud Pública, 2011).

Figure 2.16: Preferred Ways to Reduce Adolescent Alcohol and Drug Use in Tunkás

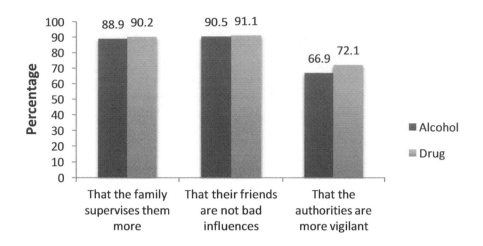

Protective factors

It is not surprising, in light of the qualitative evidence presented above, that the majority of Tunkaseños believed that parental monitoring is the key to prevention. About nine out of ten stated that increased parental supervision would reduce alcohol and drug problems among adolescents.

Numerous interviewees noted that Tunkás does not offer many opportunities that help young people achieve their dreams; consequently, one must leave Tunkás in order to get ahead. For many, improving the limited local economic opportunity structure would be the most effective way to combat adolescent alcohol and drug use. For example, interviewees mentioned that providing jobs to adolescents would reduce the need to seek employment outside of Tunkás, in places where young people are at a higher risk of being exposed to drugs and different customs. Another frequent suggestion was to provide youth with better information about educational opportunities – information that could motivate students to stay in school and pursue higher education and, as a result, stay away from alcohol and drugs. Interestingly, this hints at a unique relationship between the schools and substance abuse. If the schools point students toward further educational opportunities, and motivate them to pursue such opportunities, alcohol and drug use may decrease. If alcohol and drug use decrease, it is likely to have positive effects on educational attainment.

CONCLUSION

Despite national statistics showing that students in Mexico are completing low levels of education, our study finds that Tunkaseño youth are completing more years of schooling than ever before. Not only is the number of years of education increasing, the high school graduation rate has improved as well.

Our research suggests that a combination of family characteristics and teacher characteristics helps to explain educational attainment among Tunkaseño youth. We find that the education level of the parent, teacher expectations, and household wealth are positively associated with the number of years of schooling a young person completes. We also found that parental education, age, and household wealth are positively related to high school completion.

Educational attainment is rising among Tunkaseño youth in the face of continuing obstacles, such as inadequate school facilities, the cost of schooling, teen pregnancy, and adolescent alcohol and drug use. Alcohol and drug use among the town's youths has become a worrisome problem for teachers and parents. We find that alcohol and drugs are relatively easy for young Tunkaseños to obtain, either through *clandestinos* or known drug dealers. While some point to the migration of a parent—and the resulting potential for decreased parental supervision—as a risk factor for alcohol and drug use, others note that increased substance abuse seems to be a trend among youth regardless of the location of parents.[40] This is not to say that migration does not play a role. Indeed, many of our interviewees pointed out that migrants bring risk behaviors back to Tunkás. To reduce alcohol and drug use among adolescents, some Tunkaseños believe that "non-traditional" actions like increasing local economic opportunities may be the best approach.

Our study leads to several evidence-based recommendations that could serve to increase the educational attainment of youths in Tunkás. First, we suggest *increasing enrollment in adult school programs*. Given that parental education was not only positively associated with years of educational attainment but also with high school completion, if a parent re-enrolls in an educational program that would likely have a positive impact on the educational performance of his/her children. Parents participating in the adult school program find they are able to now help their children with their school

---

[40] For a more detailed discussion see Chapter 3 in this volume.

work in ways that were previously impossible. Furthermore, it sets an example for students of the importance of education.

A second recommendation would be *to increase collaboration between teachers and parents with regard to what the students are working on in school.* Teachers could host meetings where they review curriculum content and suggest ways in which the parents can support their children's work at home. Again, this recommendation speaks to the importance of parental education. Although learning about what their children are working on does not increase parents' levels of education, it may help them to feel better equipped to assist their children with their school work. This type of partnership can help to mediate the effects of low levels of parental education.

A third recommendation is *to encourage teachers to talk to their students more frequently about higher education, and to have these discussions earlier.* Our research suggests that teacher expectations matter. Students who graduated high school reported that their teachers held significantly higher expectations for them in terms of completing their studies compared to those who had not finished high school. Teachers must not only communicate high expectations for students more often, they must also communicate these expectations earlier in students' academic careers. One current student whom we interviewed, who was entering her last year of high school in the fall, said she would not be given information about higher education until the next school year. Given that Tunkaseños aged 15-35 complete an average of 10.8 years of education, providing information about higher education in their 12th year of schooling is too late. Providing more, and more timely, information about higher education opportunities and encouraging youths to continue their education may also lower the incidence of adolescent alcohol and drug use, because young people will have an important goal to work toward. This speaks to the special link between education and alcohol and drug use that emerged throughout our interviews. Expanding higher education opportunities will decrease the amount of alcohol and drug use in the town. With this decrease in substance abuse, educational attainment will likely rise. In other words, the outcomes are mutually reinforcing.

Another recommendation for reducing alcohol and drug use among Tunkaseño youth is to *continue information-sharing meetings between parents and teachers.* Our interviews revealed that the schools can help parents to improve their supervision of their children through parent meetings. In these meetings parents have begun to learn that some of their children were not attending school, as they believed, but rather were spending the day drinking. This sharing of information helps parents to be more aware of their child's behavior. Given our finding that supervision is a protective factor against alcohol and drug use, these parent-teacher meetings could serve as a way to communicate to children that parents *and* teachers are vigilant of their actions.

Finally, schools can help to improve supervision of children in families where a parent is absent due to migration. Our survey data show that children with a migrant parent may feel abandoned, neglected, and different from their peers. These negative feelings can predispose them to alcohol and drug abuse and lead to poor academic outcomes. Schools could provide mentors in the form of teachers, trusted community members, or older students to work with students who may be struggling with the absence of a parent. By providing another level of support for students (and their parents), there is an increase in supervision and accountability.

AGENDA FOR FUTURE RESEARCH

Although our study sheds light on the factors influencing educational attainment of rural Mexican youth and the obstacles they confront, further research is needed to address the limitations of our work. Although we did not find a statistically significant relationship between parental migration and a child's educational attainment, we caution against concluding that the migration of a parent is not important in explaining the educational attainment. Our measure of parent migration only enables us to look at children who had a parent who was living outside of Tunkás at the time of our survey— previous migration experiences are not included. A measure that captures whether a child has had, at any point in their schooling, a parent living outside of Tunkás is important to develop and include in any model to explain educational attainment.

Another important type of data that should be included in future analyses is personal alcohol and drug use. The evidence that we presented on alcohol and drug use among Tunkaseño adolescents came from questions asking about *community* perceptions. While alcohol and drug use was, indeed, perceived as a constraint on educational attainment in Tunkás, a measure of personal alcohol and drug use is needed. By incorporating such a measure into models of educational attainment, researchers can determine directly whether there is a statistically significant relationship between these risk behaviors and educational outcomes.

Finally, while our fieldwork included interviews conducted both in Tunkás and its satellite communities in southern California, we were unable to conduct systematic analysis of the educational attainment of Tunkaseños who had been schooled primarily in the United States; there were too few individuals in our sample who fit this description. By increasing the sample of U.S.-based migrants in the 15-35-year cohort, future researchers will be able to compare the educational outcomes of the same generational cohort on both sides of the border. They could also identify any differences in the factors that help to explain educational attainment in migrant-sending and receiving communities.

REFERENCES CITED

Aguila, E., Mejia, N., Perez-Arce, F., Ramirez, E., & Rivera, A. (2015). Pobreza y vulnerabilidad en México: El caso de los jóvenes que no estudian ni trabajan . *Estudios Económicos, 30*(1): 3–49.

Bakker, J., Denessen, E., & Brus-Laeven, M. (2007). Socio-economic background, parental involvement and teacher perceptions of these in relation to pupil achievement. *Educational Studies, 33*(2): 177-92.

Blair, S., Blair, M., & Madama, A. (1999). Racial/ethnic differences in high school students' academic performance: Understanding the interweave of social class and ethnicity in the family context. *Journal of Comparative Family Studies, 30*(3): 539-55.

Bogenschneider, K. (1997). Parental involvement in adolescent schooling: A proximal process with transcontextual validity. *Journal of Marriage and Family, 59*(3): 718-33.

Bordua, D. (1960). Educational aspirations and parental stress on college. *Social Forces, 38*(3): 262-69.

Borges, G., et al. (2007). The effect of migration to the United States on substance use disorders among returned Mexican migrants and families of migrants. *American Journal of Public Health*, 97(10): 1847–51. doi: 10.2105/AJPH.2006.097915

Brophy, J. (2010). *Motivating students to learn* (3rd ed.). New York, NY: Routledge.

Carrillo, A. L. (2009). The costs of success: Mexican American identity performance within culturally coded classrooms and educational achievement. *Southern California Review of Law and Social Justice*, 18(3): 641-76.

Chakravarthy, B., Shah, S., & Lotfipour, S. (2013). Adolescent drug abuse: Awareness & prevention. *The Indian Journal of Medical Research, 137*(6): 1021-23.

Chiquiar, D. & Hanson, G. (2005). International migration, self-selection, and the distribution of wages: Evidence from Mexico and the United States. *Journal of Political Economy, 113*(2): 239-81.

Cohen, E. (1965). Parental factors in educational mobility. *Sociology of Education, 38*(5): 405-25.

Coordinación Nacional de Prospera Programa de Inclusión Social (2014a). *Objeto, misión y visión.* Retrieved from https://www.prospera.gob.mx/Portal/wb/Web/objeto_mision_vision

Coordinación Nacional de Prospera Programa de Inclusión Social (2014b). *¿Qué significa?*. Retrieved from: https://www.prospera.gob.mx/Portal/wb/Web/que_significa

Ellis, R. & Lane, W. (1963). Structural supports for upward mobility. *American Sociological Review*, *28*(5): 743-56.

Greenblatt, J. (2000). Patterns of alcohol use among adolescents and associations with emotional and behavioral problems (Office of Applied Studies Working Paper). Retrieved from http://eric.ed.gov/?id=ED448387

Gutiérrez, A., & Sher, L. (2015). Alcohol and drug use among adolescents: An educational overview. *International Journal of Adolescent Medicine and Health*, 27(2): 207-12.

Halpern-Manners, A. (2011) The effect of family member migration on education and work among nonmigrant youth in Mexico. *Demography*, 48(1): 73-99.

Heyneman, S,. & Loxley, W. (1983). The effect of primary-school quality of academic achievement across twenty-nine high- and low-income countries. *American Journal of Sociology*, 88(6): 1162-94.

Instituto Nacional de Salud Pública. (2011). *Encuesta Nacional de Adiciones 2011*. Retrieved from http://encuestas.insp.mx/ena/ena2011.html#.VXiyA1LCeR8

Kahl, J. (1953). Educational and occupational aspirations of 'common man' boys. *Harvard Educational Review*, 23(3): 186-203.

Kandel, B., & Lesser, G. (1969). Parental and peer influences on educational plans of adolescents. *American Sociological Review*, 34(2): 213-223.

Kandel, W., & Kao, G. (2001). The impact of temporary labor migration on Mexican children's educational aspirations and performance. *International Migration Review 35*(4), 1205-1231.

Kandel, W. & Massey, D. (2002). The culture of Mexican migration: A theoretical and empirical analysis. *Social Forces 80*, 981-1004.

Kozol, J. (2005). *Shame of a nation: The restoration of apartheid schooling in America.* New York, NY: Three Rivers Press.

Lippold, M., Greenberg, M., Graham, J., & Feinberg, M. (2014).Unpacking the effect of parental monitoring on early adolescent problem behavior: Mediation by parental knowledge and moderation by parent-youth warmth. *Journal of Family Issues*, 35(13): 1800-23.

Mier, M., Rocha, T. & and Rabell Romero, C. (2003). Inequalities in Mexican children's schooling. *Journal of Comparative Family Studies*, 34(3): 435-54.

Mwamwenda, T., & Mwamwenda B. (1987). School facilities and pupils' academic achievement. *Comparative Education, 23*(2): 225-35.

McKenzie, D., & Rapoport, H. (2006). Can migration reduce educational attainment? Evidence from Mexico. World Bank Policy Research Working Paper No. 3952. Washington, DC: World Bank.

National Center on Addiction and Substance Abuse at Columbia University (2001). *Malignant neglect: Substance abuse and America's Schools.* New York, NY: Columbia University.

Nobles, J. (2011). Parenting from abroad: Migration, nonresident father involvement, and children's education in Mexico. *Journal of Marriage and Family, 73*: August, 729-46. doi: 10.1111/j.1741-3737.2011.00842.2

Organisation for Economic Co-operation and Development. (2014). *Education at a Glance 2014: Mexico Country Note.* Paris: OECD Publishing. doi: http://dx.doi.org/10.1787/eag-2014-en

Organisation for Economic Co-operation and Development. (2015). Do teacher-student relations affect students' well-being at school? *PISA in Focus,* No.50. Paris: OECD Publishing. doi: http://dx.doi.org/10.1787/5js391zxjjf1-en

Paat, Y. (2014) Family and community determinants of educational attainment in Mexico. *Child & Youth Services, 35*(1): 65-87. doi:10.1080/01459352.2014.893749

Palafox, J., Prawda, J. & Velez, E. (1994). Primary school quality in Mexico. *Comparative Education Review, 38*(2): 167-180

Rehberg, R., & Westby, D. (1967). Parental encouragement, occupation, education and family size: Artifactual or independent determinants of adolescent educational expectations? *Social Forces, 45*(3): 362- 374.

Rojas, H. (2014, June 20). Analfabetismo en México, una realidad de alto riesgo. *Educación Futura.* Retrieved from http://www.educacionfutura.org/analfabetismo-en-mexico-una-realidad-de-alto-riesgo/

Rosenthal, R., & Jacobson, L. (1968). *Pygmalion in the classroom: Teacher expectation and pupils' intellectual development.* New York, NY: Holt, Rinehart and Winston, Inc.

Sandefur, G., Meier, A., & Campbell, M. (2006). Family resources, social capital, and college attendance. *Social Science Research, 35*(2): 525-533. doi:10.1016/j.ssresearch.2004.11.003

Santibañez, L., Vernez, G. & Razquin, P. (2005). *Education in Mexico: Challenges and opportunities.* Santa Monica, CA: RAND Corporation.

Sawyer, A. (2013). The schooling of youth impacted by migration: A binational case study. Pp. 189-212 in B. Jensen & A. Sawyer, eds., *Regarding Educación: Mexican American Schooling, Immigration, and Binational Improvement.* New York: NY: Teachers College Press.

Sawyer, A. (2014). Is money enough?: The effect of migrant remittances on the parental aspirations and youth educational attainment in rural Mexico. *International Migration Review*, 2 September: 1-36. Doi: 10.1111/imre.12103

Sawyer, A., Keyes, D., Velásquez, C., Lima, G., & Bautista, M. (2009). Going to school, going to *El Norte*: Migration's impact of Tlacotepense education. Pp. 123-64 in Cornelius, W., FitzGerland, D., Hernández-Díaz, J. & Borger, S., eds., *Migration from the Mexican Mixteca: A Transnational Community in Oaxaca and California.* La Jolla, CA: Center for Comparative Immigration Studies, University of California, San Diego.

Silva, T., Chang, C., Osuna, C., & Solís Sosa, I. (2010). Leaving to learn or learning to leave: Education in Tunkás. Pp. 131-58 in Cornelius, W., FitzGerald, D., Lewin Fischer, P., & Muse-Orlinoff, L., eds. *Mexican Migration and the U.S. Economic Crisis: A Transnational Perspective.* La Jolla, CA: Center for Comparative Immigration Studies, University of California, San Diego.

Skinner, E., & Belmont, M. (1993). Motivation in the classroom: reciprocal effects of teacher behavior and student engagement across the school year. *Journal of Educational Psychology,* 85(4): 571-81.

Strodtbeck, F. (1958). Family interaction, values, and achievement. Pp. 135-94 in McClelland, D., et al., eds. *Talent and Society: New Perspectives in the Identification of Talent.* New York, NY: Van Nostrand.

Tavani, C., & Losh, S. (2003). Motivation, self-confidence, and expectations as predictors of the academic performances among our high school students. *Child Study Journal,* 33(3): 141-51.

Thompson, R., Lizardi, D., Keyes, K., & Hasin, D. (2008). Childhood or adolescent parental divorce/separation, parental history of alcohol problems, and offspring lifetime alcohol dependence. *Drug and Alcohol Dependence*, 98(3), 264-269.doi: 10.1016/j.drugalcdep.2008.06.011.

United Nations Development Programme. (2013). *Mean years of schooling (of adults)* [data set]. Retrieved from: http://hdr.undp.org/en/content/mean-years-schooling-adults-years

World Bank. (2015). Adolescent fertility rate (births per 1,000 women ages 15-19). Data set retrieved from: http://data.worldbank.org/indicator/SP.ADO. TFRT/countries/1W?display=default

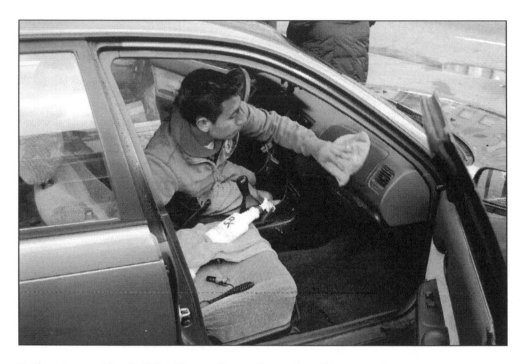

Tunkaseños working in U.S. cities are frequently employed in car washes.
(Photo by Alpha Martell)

3

What Price for Work and Friends? – Occupational Context, Social Networks, and Substance Use among Yucateco Migrants in the United States[41]

ISABEL HAVILAND DE LEÓN, TERESITA ROCHA JIMÉNEZ, PEDRO LEWIN-FISCHER, AND MARÍA LUISA ZÚÑIGA

As reported in Chapter 2 of this volume, alcohol and drug use, especially among adolescents, has become a significant concern in Tunkás. The town's adults perceive the absence of a parent due to migration as a contributor to youth initiation into these substances or increased consumption of them. Among respondents in our 2015 survey, 82 percent believed that teenagers have a higher probability of alcohol use when a parent migrates to the United States., and 79.4 percent believed that the absence of a migrant father is one of the factors that may increase vulnerability to drug use among adolescents. Nearly nine of ten respondents considered family supervision to be a key protective factor against alcohol use, and a similar proportion believed that adolescents' interaction with "bad friends" is a risk factor for alcohol use. Previous research among Tunkaseños found that migrants are at higher risk for drug and alcohol consumption when they migrate to the United States (Pinedo, et al., 2014).

These findings motivated us to explore the risk situation among U.S.-based migrants who originated in Tunkás. In this chapter we focus on the role played by workplace-based pressures and by new social networks formed by migrants in the United

---

[41]This chapter was translated from the Spanish by Miguel Pinedo and Greta Díaz. We thank Dr. Pinedo, Professor Seth Holmes, and Professor Debra Cornelius for comments on an earlier version of this chapter.

States in substance use.[42] Our central research question was: Are alcohol and drug use among working U.S. migrants associated with their limited employment options and their lifestyle in the United States? We devote special attention to migrants' condition of detachment from their home community, which creates an environment in the receiving community in which migrants become prone to the use of substances.

We begin this chapter with a review of previous research on migration, mental health, and substance use. We then describe migrants' working and living conditions in the United States. We discuss the specific risk factors to which migrants are exposed as a result of separation from their home community and the trials of the migration process itself. We focus on the migrants' adaptation to the destination city and workplace, the impact of wage labor and access to a relatively stable (and higher) income, and how these factors influence substance use. Finally, we explore what happens when migrants return to their home community in Mexico, where they may function as transfer agents for consumption and spending patterns related to substance use.

LITERATURE REVIEW

Previous research has established that migration is associated with a variety of risk factors influencing the physical and mental health of migrants in the United States (Alegría et al., 2007; Bach, 2003; Bhugra, 2004; Castañeda, et al., 2014; Ortega, et al., 2000). Separation from immediate family members, negative experiences while crossing the border, job instability, low income, drastic changes in language and culture, and social isolation are all factors that place migrants in conditions of heightened vulnerability (Salgado, et al., 2007). Some of these factors translate into increased risk of substance use, which acts as an escape valve for stressors that migrants face (Borges, et al., 2007; Medina-Mora, Breslau, & Aguilar-Gaxiola, 2007; Borges et al., 2009; Valdez et al., 2010)). Some empirical studies emphasize the co-morbidity of poor mental health and substance use in migration contexts (Breslau, et al., 2011; Ojeda, et al., 2011; Ortega, et al., 2000; Szapocznik, et al., 2007). However, there is a paucity of information about the impact of migration on mental health and the specific conditions that promote substance use among indigenous migrants.

Most studies on Mexican migration to the United States have focused on *mestizo*

---

[42]In this chapter, substance use is defined as the use of alcohol as well as hard and soft drugs.

populations (i.e. populations of mixed, indigenous and Spanish heritage). However, more recent indigenous migration flows have changed the cultural profile of Mexican migration to the United States. Since the 1990s, indigenous migrants have been the most rapidly growing segment of recently arrived Mexicans in the United States (Fox & Rivera-Salgado, eds., 2004; Lyman, et al., 2007). Indigenous migrants constitute a large portion of the 6.5 million of undocumented Mexicans estimated to be living in the United States (Passel & D'Vera, 2011). As undocumented migrants, they live frequently in structurally vulnerable circumstances (Holmes, 2011; Quesada, Hart, & Bourgois, 2011).

Previous studies have considered the influence of structural and personal attributes such as working conditions (Chen, et al., 2008), ethnicity (Organista, 2007; Vega et al., 1998), and the stressful acculturation process (Shedlin, et al., 2005) as risk factors for poor mental health, substance use, and other risk behaviors in migrant populations. Borges et al. (2009) found that substance use was more common among migrants who work in the agricultural and service sectors, although they did not delve into the specific causes and implications of this phenomenon. Sánchez-Huesca et al. (2006) explored the relationship between drug use and long working hours, emphasizing the use of stimulant drugs (cocaine and methamphetamine) as a resource to achieve higher work productivity (Sánchez-Huesca & Arellanez-Hernández, 2011).

Other studies have identified unaccompanied journeys, loneliness, lack of social support, family separation, deportation, and undocumented status as risk factors for heavy drinking among Mexican and other Latino migrants (Alderete, et al., 2000; Prelat & Maciel, 2007; Brower et al., 2009; Borges et al., 2007; Vega et al., 1998; Escobar, 1998). Internal migration (especially to tourist cities within Mexico) has also been implicated in substance use behavior (Pinedo, et al., 2015).

METHODOLOGY

This chapter is based on 42 qualitative, semi-structured interviews conducted in Spanish in 2012 and 2015.[43] Thirty of these interviews were done in Tunkás and the remainder in the southern California cities of Anaheim and Inglewood. All but one interviewee (the wife of a migrant) were men, reflecting the traditional profile of

---

[43]We wish to thank Juan Torre Valdez and Juan Rodríguez de la Gala Gómez for their contributions to the 2012 phase of this research. They conducted interviews with migrants in both Tunkás and southern California.

migration from Tunkás to the United States. About two-thirds of Tunkaseños who go north are males, most of them under 40 years of age (Martell, Pinedo, & Tapia 2007: 50). We also interviewed key informants whose views helped us gain a better understanding of the context of substance use among Tunkaseños, both in Tunkás and California. All interviews were digitally recorded and transcribed.

Subjects for qualitative interviews were a subset of respondents to the standardized survey questionnaire that was administered in Tunkás and California. Interviewees must have been born in Tunkás or were the offspring of persons born there. Additional eligibility criteria included at least one of the following: (1) having a high score (16 points or more) on the Depression Scale of the Center of Epidemiologic Studies (CES-D), which was a section of the standardized survey questionnaire administered in Tunkás in 2012;[44] (2) obtaining a high score (above 50 percent) in their responses to questions on alcohol and drug use, taken from the Alcohol Use Disorders Identification Test (AUDIT).[45]

Our analysis focuses on the intersection between substance use and mental health outcomes. We followed the general definition of mental health proposed by the World Health Organization: "a state of complete physical, mental and social well-being … in which the individual realizes his or her own abilities, can cope with everyday stress, can work in a productive and fruitful way, and is capable to make a contribution to his or her community" (World Health Organization, 2013).

Our coding taxonomy for analyzing qualitative interview data followed Bronfebrenner's model of ecological human development, subsequently adapted by

---

[44]The MMFRP's 2012 survey in Tunkás found that 7.1 percent of residents exhibited depression according to the CES-D scale. While this incidence is not very high, it was higher among interviewees with migration experience.

[45]The AUDIT questionnaire was developed by the World Health Organization to identify people with significant alcohol consumption risk. Using the resulting data it is possible to classify respondents into three categories: alcohol dependence, harmful consumers, or consumers at risk According to our 2012 standardized survey in Tunkás, 8 percent of residents were at high risk of being classified as alcohol- dependent and 14 percent were harmful consumers, indicating that consumption of alcohol is part of everyday life. Regarding drug use, the survey found that 12 percent had used marijuana in the preceding six months, 7 percent had used cocaine, 3 percent used tranquilizers, and 2 percent had used amphetamines. Eleven percent of interviewees reported that it had been in the United States that they used drugs for the first time.

Dahlberg and Krug (2002).[46] We applied the model to interpret the behavior of substance use and mental health among migrants, taking into account the influence of factors that are external to the individual. Interpersonal factors include migrants' statements about their relationships with family members and social networks of which they are part of; community expectations and norms surrounding the migrant; and structural factors including economic and labor issues, and conditions resulting from the legal status of immigrants. To identify and codify the presence of mental health issues in our interviews, we used an operational definition including depressive symptoms covered mostly by the CES-D scale, which were used for initial identification of potential qualitative interviewees.

Based on a preliminary review of our interview transcripts, as well as assessment of the language and local terms used to refer to mental and health problems, our research team identified four negative factors at the individual level that were associated with mental health problems: *loneliness* (including feeling alone, not having someone to talk to, isolation, and missing their family/community); *sadness* (including hopelessness, frustration and crying); *depression* (including statements like "being depressed," "being a failure," feelings of being discriminated against or rejected, having pessimistic thoughts, manifesting eating disorders, and psycho-somatization), and *fear or paranoia*. We also identified a positive factor for individual mental health, expressed as satisfaction with one's life after having migrated and perceived achievements in the United States. The presence of any one of these mental health-related factors served as the basis for our coding for mental health. To identify the issues related to substance use, we differentiated between alcohol use, soft drugs (marijuana, hashish) and the use of hard drugs (cocaine, methamphetamines, heroine, among others). Our analysis focused on interviewees' statements that showed the *interrelationship* between mental health and substance use issues. We excluded cases in which substance use or mental health was mentioned independently.

For the interpersonal level of our conceptual model, we identified a series of factors related to the role of the family in the life of the individual, e.g., statements about the absence of a family member as a risk factor for mental health problems or substance use. For the community level, we focused primarily on the role that social networks have

---

[46] This model was proposed as a framework for preventive actions in contexts of violence. It includes four levels: individual, interpersonal, community, and social.

in migrants' lives. Finally, for the structural level we identified labor and socioeconomic factors, the immigration status of migrants, and the sociocultural segregation perceived by migrants in the United States.

ANALYSIS

We begin this section by describing the social context of migration, devoting particular attention to the elements that make the migrant more vulnerable to substance use. We then turn to an in-depth exploration of labor conditions in the migrant's destination and how they influence substance use. Finally, we discuss the role of the returned migrant as an agent who transfers new patterns of spending and consumption, especially regarding substance use.

Vulnerability and Migration

Motivated by a search for better-paid work, the migrant leaves his community of origin in Mexico, undergoes a separation from his relatives and friends, and focuses almost entirely on finding work. Separation from family and friends can cause stress and poor mental health, as well as greater likelihood of substance use, as the following account illustrates:

> Why [do migrants consume alcohol]? First, because of loneliness. Most of the people who go [to the United States] go alone. By "alone" I mean without their wives or mothers. You have friends, right, and you have colleagues. But if you're married you remember your children, your wife. If you are unmarried, you remember your mother, your father, your little siblings. That feeling is what makes you grab that nostalgia and have an abundance of beer and everything. Sometimes they even get into drugs.
>
> -- *international returned migrant in Tunkás*

This returned migrant's testimony presents the separation of the migrant from his family as something that summons painful emotions ("nostalgia," "loneliness") that the interviewee clearly links to the use of alcohol and other drugs.

Cultural differences between the community of origin and the receiving community also contribute to poor mental health. Lack of familiarity with the culture, the language, and the lifestyle of the host community can be aggravating to the migrant's mental health (Shedlin, et al., 2005), as well as a motivating factor for

102

substance use. The migrant's precarious economic situation can exacerbate the effects of culture shock, since in many cases there can be no return to the home community until enough money is saved to repay the debts he incurred in order to hire a people-smuggler and cover other costs of migrating. These debts typically take the form of loans from relatives based in the United States. The following comment is illustrative:

> One drinks and feels lonely, depressed, and doesn't know what to do. I went out there on the streets, and even though there were thousands of people I felt alone. You can't talk to anyone. When I arrived there were hardly any Mexicans. I couldn't even buy food. I didn't know how to ask for it. I was like that for about three months, but since I paid a lot of money to go, I said, if I go back now, how will I repay it?

> -- *international returned migrant in Tunkás*

This interviewee also stresses the feelings of loneliness, depression, and impotence that stem from cultural isolation and linguistic barriers, leading to alcohol use.

Another factor that contributes to a sense of vulnerability among migrants is their lack of legal status in the United States, a condition affecting most migrants from Tunkás. It is well established that undocumented status is one of the main causes of worry, stress, paranoia, and anxiety among migrants (Holmes, 2013; Crocker, 2015). The following testimony illustrates the negative effects of legal status on the emotional state of the interviewee:

> We feel frustrated because of the scoldings we get in our jobs. We just have to suck it up. That's the way they treat us because we don't have papers. They made fun of me, and it made me angry. I would always arrive angry because I saw the money that waiters made.

> -- *current undocumented migrant in Inglewood, CA*

This account illustrates the situation of an unauthorized migrant who suffers from an absence of labor protections. His marginalization invites contempt from his supervisors and colleagues at work and results in lower earnings, which makes him[47] angry.

Legal status is related not only to mental health issues but also to substance use. For example, an interviewee mentioned that he never received promotions at work

---

[47] Our use of the male pronoun in this chapter reflects the fact that all but one of the migrants with whom we conducted qualitative interviews were male.

because he was undocumented, and explained that this was one of the reasons he began to drink with his friends. He had lost the desire to focus on work and improve his life:

> The work stuff, the frustrations build up. I want to achieve this but I can't. I mean you want to, but the law doesn't allow it, and you begin [drinking] with your friends. Oh well, I'll just have to keep this job.
>
> *-- current undocumented migrant in Inglewood CA*

This migrant attributes his alcohol use to the unresolved conflict between his economic ambitions and his legal status in the United States. Another interviewee described the situation of one of his friends, whose fear due to undocumented status led him to consume alcohol before going to work:

> I think that there are people who drink more or do more drugs [because they are undocumented]. I had a friend who lived in fear. He was trembling. He would drink three or four beers and calm down. Then he would go to work. I think that was wrong because he worked cutting meat [as a butcher]. He could've gotten hurt!
>
> *-- domestic and international returned migrant in Tunkás*

This comment illustrates a case in which, to avoid the paralyzing fear caused by his undocumented status, the migrant prefers to risk his life drinking alcohol. Alcohol allows him to be functional and productive at work, despite having a dangerous job. The following excerpt from another interview further illustrates the sense of vulnerability resulting from undocumented status, specifically in relation to the workplace:

> They ask for your papers at hotels. I've noticed that many Tunkaseños who can't work at hotels have to work at car washes -- all those places where they don't require papers. But that's the main problem. You arrive at places where you can work, where they don't require papers, and they pay you practically whatever they want.
>
> *-- current undocumented migrant in Inglewood, CA*

Our interviews demonstrate that the vulnerability associated with undocumented status results in extremely precarious labor conditions, fewer job options, and, consequently, greater economic insecurity. These represent risk factors for the emotional

104

stability of migrants and predispose them to substance use. Additionally, undocumented status limits the ability of migrants to return to their community of origin, even for short visits with their families, because they run the risk of not being able to get back into the United States. Furthermore, the lack of medical services available to migrants who are undocumented can negatively impact their mental health and lead to substance use.

The insertion of the migrant into a U.S. community that is unfamiliar and, in many cases, is perceived as hostile restricts the individual's agency. The structural conditions of the migrant's new social context, in which the distinction between work and non-work networks is diffuse or nonexistent, make it difficult to turn down an offer of drugs or alcohol to increase productivity. Indeed, many of the decisions and behaviors of migrants in this new context are shaped by social networks anchored in the workplace, as we discuss in the following section.

The New Labor Environment: Social Networks and Substance Use

This section explores specific features of the migrant's new environments, emphasizing the importance of social networks and labor context as well as the relationship between these two factors and substance use. As discussed above, in many cases migrants cannot return to their homes in Mexico, especially if undocumented status would preclude them from (legally) re-entering the United States, or if they incurred large debts in order to migrate. This situation results in greater dependence on social networks in the U.S. receiving community. It has been well-established that social networks are key mechanisms for finding work in the migrant's destination (Adler, 2008; Cohen, 2004; Cornelius, et al., 2007; Fortuny, 2004; Massey, 1990). In previous MMFRP studies of migrants from Tunkás approximately 80 percent had been referred to their U.S. employer by a friend or relative (Martell, et al., 2007). In the current study, we observe the clear and powerful influence of social networks on migrants' mental health and substance use, particularly in the context of the workplace.

Specifically, our data suggest that people who report substance use typically did not initiate, nor continue using, purely as an act of self-will but rather due to workplace-based social pressure. The following interview responses are illustrative:

— Can you tell me about the first time you drank?

I was about eleven years old, and I was with a friend from work.

-- current international migrant, Inglewood, CA

I went to Playa del Carmen with some folks that were not from [Tunkás]. They were from Tabasco, Chiapas, and from Merida, different places.

— And you worked with them?

Yes.

— And when did you start to drink? When you were with them?

Yes, with them. I started to drink, smoke, and everything.

—You tried marijuana with them for the first time?

Yes.

—And cocaine?

Same.

-- internal returned migrant in Tunkás

— Do you think that work influenced the way you consumed substances?

Yes, due to the people I worked with. The majority who were there would go for it. After a while I decided that was not the life for me and I took off [left].

-- returned internal and international migrant in Tunkás

The first interviewee quoted above reports early initiation of alcohol use in a work context. All three interviewees show the influence of workplace-based social pressure on substance use.

Additionally, our data show that among these migrants there is a general acceptance and use of drugs in U.S. destination cities. Recent migrants are particularly vulnerable to the culture of drug use that they encounter there:

When one gets there [the United States], they give you everything.
When you are a rookie, they give you everything.

-- undocumented migrant in Inglewood, CA

When I'm with my friends drinking beers, they take [drugs] out, and
they say "you are next."

--migrant in Anaheim, CA

Given their long work hours and limited time to rest, migrants take on few activities outside of work. They rest in order to continue working. Combined with social isolation, this pattern of behavior keeps migrants tied to a cycle of work that generates considerable stress. In this context, workplace-based social networks strongly influence their lives. The social pressures emanating from these networks make migrants more likely to initiate substance use and to continue it.

Drugs, Mental Health, and Work Productivity

In this section we will explore the impact of full-time wage labor in a highly demanding U.S. work environment on substance use among migrants.[48] In such environments labor productivity is the priority. Wage labor differs from the types of work usually done in migrants' communities of origin, consisting mainly of agricultural and short-term construction work (e.g., carpentry, plumbing, electrical work) or running a family- or personally-owned business (Bracamonte, 2007; Quintal et al, 2012.). In the new U.S. environment of high labor productivity, stimulants are commonly used to increase productivity. Often, the use of drugs to enhance work performance occurs without the migrant having to deliberately seek them out. The following quotes from our interviews illustrate this pattern of behavior:

---

[48] It is important to note that in the aftermath of the Great Recession, full-time jobs in the United States are more difficult to obtain. Nevertheless, most Tunkaseño migrants working in the United States are fully employed, even if this means holding several part-time jobs (Cornelius, et al., 2010).

When I tried coke, I felt fine. It was good for [people like me] because you take one of those drugs and you get to work more…. I didn't seek it, they gave it to me.

-- *undocumented migrant in Inglewood, CA*

I'd be off from my work shift, and if I wanted to make more money my friend would give me cocaine to be able to stay awake longer. In fact we even had it at our workplace. There was a cook who would take it and sell it….I would be like a zombie. I wouldn't eat, and I became very thin. I started to have problems with my wife.

--*returned internal and international migrant in Tunkás*

In these accounts, substance use does not have a recreational purpose. Instead it is a survival strategy -- an activity that allows for increased capacity to work and therefore greater income. Drug use becomes a practice of self-destruction for self-preservation. It is a means to combat fatigue, intensify work, stay awake, and endure long working hours, as well as to deceive their fatigued bodies and minds.

An environment of consumerism and constant spending exacerbates stress brought on by faster-paced work. The following statement illustrates the differences in work life and consumption patterns between Tunkás and the United States that migrants experience:

Because there are so many things that one has to struggle with in Tunkás, you don't feel the weight of work. There is peace. You have your store, your business, you don't ask for a lot. But in this country [the United States], you pay for this, you pay for that, and there are times when you became aware that you only work to pay for things.

-- *international migrant in Inglewood CA*

Thus, working in a highly disciplined, demanding, and full-time context, coupled with the high-spending patterns that characterize life in the United States, can set the stage for the use of stimulants and threaten the mental health of migrants.

Drugs, Relaxation, a Sense of Community

In this section we explore the other side of the coin: substance use as a means to reduce the destructiveness associated with work life, and to search for a state of relaxation that can sustain productivity during the next work day. Several of our interviews suggested that alcohol is part of migrants' daily routine. They work for ten or twelve hours and at the end of the day indulge in alcohol and drug use. Excessive alcohol use at the end of the workday in the United States was common:

> In Cancún I would not drink, I would drink two, three beers when I was done with work. In the United States there were times when we were done working and would drink until you felt that you couldn't anymore. You go to sleep and that's it; the next day you go back to work....We drank more in the United States than in Cancún.
>
> *-- returned internal and international migrant in Tunkás*

Alcohol use during times of rest is an extremely common practice among Tunkaseño migrants to the United States. The following quote illustrates the "normalization" of alcohol in the homes of international migrants:

> If you see a fellow *paisano* [migrant], the first thing he does is offer you a beer....In the home of whatever *paisano* is working in the United States, in his refrigerator there may not be milk, sodas, or meat, but there is always beer.
>
> *-- returned international migrant in Tunkás*

Other interviews revealed the importance of purchasing alcohol as a way to make friendships and achieve social benefits:

> If I know that everyone likes [alcohol], and I buy and bring it, they will spend time with me. You buy friends.... Sometimes I'll go to the liquor store and I'll bring a 12-pack, and tell them, "Here it is, I know what kind you drink.
>
> *--migrant in Anaheim, CA*

In some cases, the migrant who decides not to consume alcohol finds himself isolated from his fellow migrants:

> When you stop living in that world of alcohol you lose many friends. Right now I've been without [a drink] for about two years. I have not seen one Tunkaseño during that time. Before, it was just constant drinking. The Tunkaseños would have parties, and everyone would drink.
>
> *--migrant in Inglewood, CA*

In sum, we found a close link between alcohol use and social cohesion among Tunkaseño migrants. The workplace and social networks are inseparable in the life of the migrant, and they directly influence the incidence of substance use.

Wage-earning Jobs and Access to Substances

An essential factor that facilitates migrants' access to substances in the United States is having a consistent income made possible by a wage-earning job – an income that is considerably higher than what they had in their home community. In a case where a vulnerable migrant is using stimulant drugs to be productive at work and depressive substances to rest, economic resources can be channeled to sustain this pattern. Migrants whom we interviewed reported an increase in their purchasing power as a key factor enabling them to buy substances:

> Over there, in the U.S., I worked and I had money to buy [drugs and alcohol]. But here [in Tunkás] you work but you don't make the same as over there. Over there you can buy the things that you want.
>
> *-- international returned migrant in Tunkás*

> In the U.S. most of the people work, have money, and they buy what they want -- crystal [meth], cocaine.
>
> *-- internal and international returned migrant in Tunkás*

> In the United States there are stable jobs and you have a fixed salary. Suddenly you are buying [alcohol]. Here [in Tunkás], you don't have that money and a fixed salary. In the U.S. people drink more alcohol. It's easier because there's more money.
>
> *-- international returned migrant in Tunkás*

Thus, a secure and high income (by Tunkás standards) increases the migrant's capacity to access alcohol and drugs, consumption of which often turns into a concurrent social activity and/or an addiction.

In addition, not knowing how to manage their relatively high earnings leads some migrants to spend it on substances. As several of our interviewees explained:

110

I think that the money does affect [drug use]. I didn't know what to do. I was by myself, young and with money. I would spend it on drugs.

--returned migrant in Tunkás

I used to drink more in the United States, because I had more money and I was alone. I didn't have my parents with me. There was no one to scold me and a lot of time, the loneliness gets to you. You start drinking.

-- internal and international returned migrant in Tunkás

Many migrants stressed the importance of peer pressure as a factor leading them to spend a significant proportion of their earnings on drugs, despite their desire to save as much money as possible:

I couldn't save money [because of] the alcohol… I would work and in one day I would make like $180. When you have money, then the friends are there. They would come and see me still washing cars and say, "Are we going to drink at the store over there?" And I would say, "Yes, but in a little while." I would finish washing the car and I would meet them with my money, and they would be there waiting for me.

--international migrant working at a car wash in Inglewood, CA

There were days when I would say no. I still had money and I'd save it. But if I have money and my friends start to tempt me, the more I will spend it.

-- internal and international returned migrant in Tunkás

When [migrants] have money, they go and buy beer all the time. I said no, and they told me to go away, or they would say, "Look, are you a faggot or something? Are you chickening out?" There is always a friend who bullies you.

-- internal and international returned migrant in Tunkás

Thus, substance use emerges as a social prestige marker – a way to attract people, exert influence on them, and acquire recognition. The third interviewee quoted above also refs to virility discourses ("Are you a faggot or something?") that migrants may employ to put pressure on their peers to use substances.

Return Migrants' Contribution to Changes in Spending and Consumption Patterns

Previous research has shown that migrants returning home from the United States, and their relatives, are at greater risk of substance use than non-migrants (Borges, et al., 2007, 2009; Sánchez-Huesca, et al., 2011). For example, return migrants have a higher probability of having used alcohol, marijuana, or cocaine in their lifetime and during the previous twelve months. They also have a greater likelihood of developing a pattern of substance abuse than the general population (Borges, et al. 2007). Additionally, substance use is more common among return migrants who have lived in the United States for longer periods of time (Borges, et al., 2009; Sánchez-Huesca, et al., 2011). In this section we will explore the potential influence that return migrants may have on substance use patterns in their community of origin.

Experience living as a migrant in the United States may give returnees disproportionate influence on substance use behavior in one's home town. The returned migrant brings the prestige of having experienced life outside the community, as well as the economic resources to access drugs and alcohol. The following comment illustrates how returned migrants are perceived by many Tunkaseños:

> Migrants consume more alcohol. I don't know why they do it; could be habits that they picked up over there. They return and have more money than the rest of us. Someone who has been here all the time earning 70 pesos a day doesn't have the luxury of going to a *cantina*. And one who comes from the U.S. with their savings of three, four, five thousand dollars, one almost always sees them with their beer and with drugs.
>
> *-- non-migrant in Tunkás*

Similarly, the returned migrant may induce other members of his home community to adopt his practices, among them drug use:

> Those who have gone and returned are the ones who already know how to get it [drugs], how to consume it. They'll tell you, "Look, try this, this is how you do it, this is how you consume it." When one is naïve and does not know much, they quickly get you involved. And because one wants to be like them, you say, "Oh yes, I want this too." It's rare that one starts using here; it comes from outside.
>
> *-- returned migrant from the United States in Tunkás*

112

This narrative demonstrates the ease with which returned migrants can influence cultural practices in the community of origin, particularly involving substance use. It also presents the returned migrant as someone who has certain knowledge that non-migrant residents do not possess—in this case, knowledge related to obtaining and consuming drugs. The returned migrant emerges as an individual with access to knowledge and who is admired because of his experience outside the community. Moreover, as noted above, the returned migrant has greater access to economic resources, which in turn enhances his power to serve as a vector in the transmission of practices related to substance use in his home community.

CONCLUSIONS AND RECOMMENDATIONS

Our study suggests that the risky use of alcohol and drugs is associated with structural factors, such as lack of legal status in the United States, that increase vulnerability and cause higher levels of stress. In terms of interpersonal relationships, norms of reciprocity and expectations generated by workplace-based social networks also exert an influence on illicit substance use. We found that migrants' vulnerability to substance use in the United States is compounded by the need to cope with demanding work schedules that lend themselves to self-medication with substances. Moreover, feelings of sadness, loneliness, and depression that migrants reported, caused largely by separation from close relatives, encourage greater dependence on friendship networks that facilitate consumption of substances as a social obligation.

Some researchers argue that there are multiple factors that protect migrants against drug use. According to the migrants themselves, these factors include education, family, values, and traditions -- elements that give migrants a sense of their own self-worth and the value of their collective roots (Sánchez-Huesca et al., 2011). Several of our migrant interviewees reported that they did not use drugs or alcohol at home, in the presence of family members, if those relatives were present in the United States. Protective factors like the maintenance of family relationships and the support of activities associated with cultural traditions (e.g., baseball teams consisting of players from the migrant's home town) may be important in reducing the incidence of substance use among migrants and protecting their mental health.

The findings of our study reveal a restriction on individual decision-making that promotes substance use. As we are reminded by Paul Farmer (2003), the decisions of many persons are limited by racism, sexism, political violence, and extreme poverty. These limitations are further influenced by the relationships that migrants create and maintain through workplace-based social networks, as well as by immigration laws and policies that limit their economic opportunities. We found that Tunkaseño migrants in the United States tend to hold jobs requiring them to be highly productive and to tolerate very long work schedules. We found that drugs are often used to assist the migrant worker to maintain this demanding work cycle.

Our study, as well as previous research (Zúñiga, et al., 2014; Pinedo, et al., 2015), found an acute awareness among some members of a community of emigration concerning the impacts of migration, not only in an economic sense but also in terms of mental health consequences. These critical perceptions among certain community residents should be considered in developing interventions to mitigate the harmful effects of migration on substance use behaviors and mental health problems, in both migrant-sending and receiving communities.

Future studies could further explore economic decision-making processes among migrants, specifically, spending for the purchase of drugs and alcohol. Greater attention should also be devoted to the role of social networks in moderating – not just encouraging -- the use of substances. Thus it would be possible to think of interventions that seek to change substance use patterns through better management of U.S. earnings that are high in relation to incomes earned in the home community. Of course, the potential benefits of macro-structural interventions like improvement of working conditions for migrant workers and comprehensive immigration reform should not be overlooked.

Our study focused on a group of indigenous migrants of Mayan origin. Cultural beliefs and practices that are specific to Maya communities can be useful in explaining mental health and substance use problems and should be incorporated into future research. For example, applying standardized questionnaires may underestimate the prevalence of mental health problems like depression in an indigenous population. Thus, recent findings concerning symptoms of, and mechanisms for coping with, poor mental health in the Mayan culture can be useful to redirect future research and develop interventions that are culturally relevant (Jiménez, 2008).

To support community members in improving their ability to handle the stressors they face when migrating or returning from the United States, as well as to reduce their vulnerability to risky consumption of alcohol or drugs, it is essential that researchers, health practitioners, and public decision-makers seek long-term involvement in both migrant-sending and migrant-receiving communities. Thus, we suggest that future studies take into account the advantages of participatory research strategies, which allow the development of interventions that are informed by the voice and participation of the same people who will directly benefit from these interventions, both migrants and their families.

LIMITATIONS

Having employed a qualitative approach, this study has some important limitations. The first relates to the size of the sample. Given the small number of interviewees, our results may not be generalizable to migrants originating in other parts of Mexico. However, our findings are consistent with those of other studies that identify mechanisms of adaptation to high-risk behaviors among Mexican migrants to the United States (e.g., Sánchez-Huesca, et al., 2012).

Since our study is not longitudinal, we lack information on the mental health conditions and substance use behaviors of persons before they migrated. This makes it harder to assess whether migrants had certain patterns of behavior before migrating (for example, a predisposition to high levels of alcohol consumption). A longitudinal study would illustrate more clearly the initiation of substance use as well as changes in substance use patterns and the mental health of migrants, by providing comparative data before and after migration and facilitating causal inferences.

Finally, all but one of the migrants with whom we conducted qualitative interviews were males. A study that included more women, both migrants and non-migrants, could provide significant information for understanding of the effects of migration on substance use and mental health. Notwithstanding these limitations, we believe that our research can serve as a point of departure for future studies that will deepen our understanding of the effects of migration on substance use and help to identify possible stages and forms of intervention to mitigate the effects of the pressures and restrictions that migrants experience.

REFERENCES CITED

Adelman, M., Haldane, H., & Wies, J. (2012). Mobilizing culture as an asset: A transdisciplinary effort to rethink gender violence. *Violence against Women,* 18(6): 691-700.

Adler, R. (2008) *Yucatecans in Dallas, Texas,* 2nd ed. Boston, MA: Pearson/Allyn & Bacon.

Alderete, E., Vega, W., Kolody, B., & Aguilar-Gaxiola, S. (2000). Lifetime prevalence of and risk factors for psychiatric disorders among Mexican migrant farmworkers in California. *American Journal of Public Health,* 90(4): 608-14.

Alegría, M., Mulvaney-Day, N., Torres, M., Polo, A., Cao, Z., & Canino, G. (2007). Prevalence of psychiatric disorders across Latino subgroups in the United States. *American Journal of Public Health,* 97(1): 68-75. doi: 10.2105/AJPH.2006.087205

Bach, S. (2003). International migration of health workers: Labour and social issues. Geneva: International Labour Office.

Bhugra, D. (2004). Migration and mental health. *Acta Psychiatrica Scandinavica,* 109(4): 243-258.

Borges, G., Medina-Mora, M., Breslau, J., & Aguilar-Gaxiola, S. (2007). The effect of migration to the United States on substance use disorders among returned Mexican migrants and families of migrants. *American Journal of Public Health,* 97(10): 1847-51.

Borges, G., Medina-Mora, M. E., Orozco, R., Fleiz, C., Cherpitel, C., & Breslau, J. (2009). Mexican migration to the United States and substance use in northern Mexico. *Addiction,* 104(4): 603-11.

Bracamonte, P. (2007). *Una deuda histórica: Ensayo sobre las condiciones de pobreza secular entre los mayas de Yucatán.* México, D.F.: CIESAS.

Breslau, J., Borges, G., Tancredi, D., Saito, N., Kravitz, R., Hinton, L., et al. (2011). Migration from Mexico to the United States and subsequent risk for depressive and anxiety disorders: A cross-national study. *Archives of General Psychiatry,* 68(4): 428-33.

Brouwer, K., Lozada, R., Cornelius, W., Cruz, M., Magis-Rodriguez, C., De Nuncio, M., et al. (2009). Deportation along the U.S.–Mexico border: Its relation to drug use patterns and accessing care. *Journal of Immigrant and Minority Health,* 11(1): 1-6.

Castañeda, H., Holmes, S., Madrigal, D., De Trinidad-Young, M., Beyeler, N., & Quesada, J. (2014). Immigration as a social determinant of health. *Annual Review of Public Health*, 36(1). doi: 10.1146/annurev-publhealth-032013-182419

Chen, X., Stanton, B., Li, X., Fang, X., & Lin, D. (2008). Substance use among rural-to-urban migrants in China: A moderation effect model analysis. *Substance Use & Misuse*, 43(1): 105-24.

Cohen, J. 2004. *The Culture of Migration in Southern Mexico*. Austin: TX: University of Texas Press.

Cornelius, W., Fitzgerald, D., & Lewin-Fischer, P. (2007). *Mayan Journeys: The New Migration from Yucatán to the United States*. La Jolla, CA: Center for Comparative Immigration Studies: University of California-San Diego.

Cornelius, W., Fitzgerald, D., Lewin-Fischer, P., & Muse-Orlinoff, L. (2010). *Mexican Migration and the U.S. Economic Crisis: A Transnational Perspective*. La Jolla, CA: Center for Comparative Immigration Studies: University of California-San Diego.

Crocker R. (2015). Emotional testimonies: An ethnographic study of emotional suffering related to migration from Mexico to Arizona. *Frontiers in Public Health*. Jul 13;3:177. doi: 10.3389/fpubh.2015.00177. eCollection 2015.

Dahlberg, L., & Krug, E. (2002). Violence: A global public health problem. Pp. 1-56 in E. Krug, L. Dahlberg, J. Mercy, A. Zwi & R. Lozano, eds., *World Report on Violence and Health*. Geneva, Switzerland: World Health Organization.

Escobar, J. (1998). Immigration and mental health: Why are immigrants better off? *Archives of General Psychiatry*, 55(9): 781-82. doi:10.1001/archpsyc.55.9.781.

Fortuny Loret de Mola, P. (2004). Transnational hetzmek: Entre Oxkutzcab y San Pancho. In J. Castillo-Cocom & Q. Castañeda, eds., *Estrategias identitarias: educación y antropología histórica en Yucatán*. Mérida, Yuc.: Universidad Pedagógica Nacional.

Fox, J., & Rivera-Salgado, G., eds. (2004) *Indigenous Mexican Migrants in the United States*. La Jolla, CA: Center for Comparative Immigration Studies, University of California-San Diego.

Holmes, S. (2011). Structural vulnerability and hierarchies of ethnicity and citizenship on the farm. *Medical Anthropology*, 30(4): 425-49.

Holmes, S. (2013) *Fresh Fruit, Broken Bodies: Migrant Farmworkers in the United States*. Berkeley, CA: University of California Press.

Jiménez, D. (2008). *Los movimientos del ánimo: Estudio sobre las concepciones entre los mayas de Felipe Carrillo Puerto, Quintana Roo*. Mérida, Yuc.: Universidad Autónoma de Yucatán.

Krug, G., Dahlberg, L., Mercy, A., Zwi, B., & Lozano, R. (2002). *World Report on Violence and Health*. Geneva, Switzerland: World Health Organization.

Lyman, B., Cen-Montuy, M., & Tejeda-Sandoval, E. (2007). Migration and ethnicity. Pp. 169-91 in W. Cornelius, P. Lewin-Fischer, & D. Fitzgerald, eds., *Mayan Journeys. The New Migration from Yucatán to the United States.* La Jolla, CA: Center for Comparative Immigration Studies, University of California-San Diego.

Martell, A., Pineda, M., & Tapia, L. (2007). The contemporary migration process. Pp. 49-70 in W. Cornelius, P. Lewin-Fischer, & D. Fitzgerald, eds., *The New Migration From Yucatan to the United States*. La Jolla, CA: Center for Comparative Immigration Studies, University of California-San Diego.

Massey, D. (1990). Social structure, household strategies, and the cumulative causation of migration. *Population Index*, 56(1): 3-26.

Ojeda, V.., Robertson, A., Hiller, S., Lozada, R., Cornelius, W., Palinkas, L., et al. (2011). A qualitative view of drug use behaviors of Mexican male injection drug users deported from the United States. *Journal of Urban Health*, 88(1): 104-17.

Organista, K. (2007). *Solving Latino Psychosocial and Health Problems: Theory, Research, and Populations:* Hoboken, NJ: Wiley & Sons.

Ortega, A., Rosenheck, R., Alegria, M., & Desai, R. (2000). Acculturation and the lifetime risk of psychiatric and substance use disorders among Hispanics. *The Journal of Nervous and Mental Disease,* 188(11): 728-35.

Passel, J., & D'Vera, C. (2011). Unauthorized immigrant population: National and state trends, 2010. Washington, DC: Pew Research Center. Retrieved from http://www.pewhispanic.org/2011/02/01/unauthorized-immigrant-population-brnational-and-state-trends-2010/

Pinedo, M., Campos, Y., Leal, D., Fregoso, J,, Goldenberg, S., Zúñiga, M. (2014). Alcohol use behaviors among indigenous migrants: A transnational study of communities of origin and destination. *Journal of Immigrant and Minority Health,* 16(3): 348-55. doi: 10.1007/s10903-013-9964-8.

Pinedo, M., Kang Sim, D., Espinoza Giacinto, R., Zúñiga, M.. (2015). An exploratory study of internal migration and substance use among an indigenous community in southern Mexico. *Family and Community Health,* in press.

Prelat, S., & Maciel, A. (2007). Migration and health. Pp. 233-48 in W. Cornelius, P. Lewin-Fischer, & D. Fitzgerald, eds., *The New Migration From Yucatan to the United States*. La Jolla, CA: Center for Comparative Immigration Studies, University of California-San Diego.

Quesada, J., Hart, L., & Bourgois, P. (2011). Structural vulnerability and health: Latino migrant laborers in the United States. *Medical Anthropology*, 30(4): 339-62.

Quintal, E., Bastarrachea, J., Briceño, F., Lewin-Fischer, P., Medina, M., Quiñones, T., Rejón, L. (2012). Mayas en movimiento: Movilidad laboral y redefinición de las comunidades mayas de la península. In M. Nolasco & M. Rubio, eds., *Movilidad migratoria de la población indígena de México: Las comunidades multilocales y los nuevos espacios de interacción social*, v. 2, México, DF: INAH-CONACULTA.

Salgado, V., González-Vázquez, T., Bojórquez, I., & Infante, C. (2007). Vulnerabilidad social, salud, y migración México-Estados Unidos. *Salud Pública de México*, 49 (special issue): 8-10.

Sánchez, M., et al. (2012). The effect of migration on HIV high-risk behaviors among Mexican migrants. *JAIDS: Journal of Acquired Immune Deficiency Syndromes*, 61(5): 610-17.

Sánchez-Huesca, R., & Arellanez-Hernández, J. (2011). Uso de drogas en migrantes mexicanos captados en ciudades de la frontera noroccidental México-Estados Unidos. *Estudios Fronterizos*, 12(23): 9-26.

Sánchez-Huesca, R., Arellanez-Hernández, J., Pérez-Islas, V., & Rodríguez-Kuri, S. (2006). Estudio de la relación entre consumo de drogas y migración a la frontera norte de México y Estados Unidos. *Salud Mental*, 29(1): 35-43.

Shedlin, M., Decena, C., Oliver-Velez, D. (2005). Initial acculturation and HIV risk among new Hispanic immigrants. *Journal of the National Medical Association*, Jul.97(7 Suppl): 32S-37S.

Szapocznik, J., Prado, G., Burlew, A., Williams, R., & Santisteban, D. (2007). Drug abuse in African American and Hispanic adolescents: Culture, development, and behavior. *Annual Review of Clinical Psychology*, 3: 77-105.

Valdez, A., Cepeda, A., Negi, N., & Kaplan, C. (2010). *Fumando la piedra*: Emerging patterns of crack use among Latino immigrant day laborers in New Orleans. *Journal of Immigrant and Minority Health*, 12(5): 737-42.

Vega, W., Kolody, B., Aguilar-Gaxiola, S., Alderete, E., Catalano, R., & Caraveo-Anduaga, J. (1998). Lifetime prevalence of DSM-III-R psychiatric disorders among urban and rural Mexican Americans in California. *Archives of General Psychiatry*, 55(9): 771.

World Health Organization (2014). Mental health: A state of well-being. *Fact Files*. Retrieved from http://www.who.int/features/factfiles/mental_health/en/

Zúñiga M., Lewin-Fischer P., Cornelius, W., Goldenberg, S., Keyes, D. (2014). A transnational approach to understanding indicators of mental health, alcohol use, and reproductive health among indigenous Mexican migrants. *Journal of Immigrant and Minority Health*, 16(3): 329-39. doi 10.1007/s10903-013-9949-7.

Tunkaseño *apicultor* (beekeeper) Raymundo Leal Mena tends his hives.

(Photo by Rodrigo Díaz Guzmán)

4

The Flowers that Wilt: Assessing Impacts of Climate Change on a Migrant Community

MANUEL AVINA, ALMA ESPARZA, AND ELIZABETH FLORES

Ever since Hurricane Gilberto came through here [in 1988] we have had problems. The fields have never produced enough to maintain my family. Sometimes the rains don't come, sometimes *la langosta* or other plagues come, and the crops never mature.

— Pedro, a 50-year-old Tunkaseño

How is the uncertainty caused by climate change affecting those who remain in migrant-sending communities and who depend on the land for their livelihoods? According to the Intergovernmental Panel on Climate Change, future impacts of climate change will be particularly acute in rural areas, and will include limited access to water, food insecurity, and declining income from agriculture (IPCC report, 19). For the next generation of farmers, the decrease in yield could be as great as 25 percent (IPCC report, 18). Already, climate change is aggravating various factors that make subsistence agriculture a difficult enterprise. The overall picture is one of increasing uncertainty for agriculturalists, which has important potential implications for residents of communities of emigration. In other words, climate change is making it increasingly difficult to predict how much and what type of effort will be needed to harvest crops, tend livestock, and otherwise extract income from the land. In this chapter, we examine the impact of climate change on Tunkaseños who derive some part of their economic livelihood from working the land. We first identify the main pathways through which climate change is increasing uncertainty associated with small-scale agriculture, then we assess the impact of this uncertainty on Tunkaseños' decisions to migrate.

Tunkás, located in the semi-arid center of Mexico's Yucatán peninsula, is a late-blooming community of emigration, historically dependent upon agriculture for subsistence and culturally tied to the land through Mayan beliefs and traditions. Agriculturalists in the town have focused on various products including henequen, wood

121

for furniture, maize, and honey. However, the delicate ecological setting has left any sort of land-related activity exposed to the whims of the climate.[49] Recent fluctuations in rainfall have increased the difficulties of making a living through agricultural activity (Cornelius et al. 2007: Chap. 2).

Is the ecosystem in Tunkás changing in ways that decrease the profitability of agriculture and the propensity of Tunkaseños to engage in agricultural activities? How has climate change affected agricultural production in Tunkás, and how has this influenced international and internal (within Mexico) migration behavior? These are the key questions addressed in this chapter. Our principal findings are that changing weather patterns have severely impacted the livelihoods of Tunkaseño farmers, and that these effects are credibly linked to the decision to migrate, both internationally and to destinations within Mexico.

We begin our analysis by drawing upon qualitative (semi-structured) interviews conducted in Tunkás. Using this evidence we find substantial and varied impacts of climate change on the town's agricultural sector. These interviews lead us to conclude that climate change has greatly increased the overall risk and uncertainty faced by Tunkaseños working in the agricultural sector. Second, using the results of our standardized survey interviews, we demonstrate potential links between climate and the decision to migrate. We find that higher levels of difficulty in extracting value from agricultural land are associated with an increased likelihood of international migration. Somewhat surprisingly, we also demonstrate that families who work the land have a *lower* likelihood of migrating to other places within Mexico. In our discussion section, we offer an explanation of these findings based on the uncertainty faced by rural migrants.

The chapter proceeds as follows. In the next section, we review the literature on climate change, its association with crop loss, and its effects on migration. In the following section, we detail the specific impacts of climate change on both crop production and honey production (bee keeping) in Tunkás. We then turn to an analysis of

---

[49]According to a study by Cohen et al. (2013), the Mayan Empire collapsed because of the over-exploitation of scarce water resources, irregular precipitation, and fragile biodiversity in the Yucatán peninsula.

the link between agriculture and migration decisions. Finally, we discuss the implications of our results for this young and increasingly important subfield of migration studies.

CLIMATE CHANGE, AGRICULTURE, AND MIGRATION

Climatic changes have led to increasing agricultural losses and a greater need to migrate. As demonstrated by the IPCC's climate change reports, each of the last three decades has been successively warmer at the Earth's surface than any preceding decade since 1850. Global average land and ocean surface temperature has increased by 0.85 degrees Celsius over the last 30 years (IPCC 2014a: 2).

Climatic changes are taking a toll on agricultural production, one that demands increased adaptability while also potentially increasing migration. Liverman and O'Brian (1991) assert that climatic changes within Mexico could reduce moisture in the soil, causing great devastation to most Mexican cropland and especially to those farmers who rely on rainfall. They suggest that while the most critical stressor for farmers is variability in climate, the decrease in soil fertility and fallow periods[50] also impedes successful crop growth. Overall, it is believed that the loss of production is due to either droughts or frosts that destroy crops. This conclusion is further supported by the 2014 IPCC report, which summarizes studies conducted over a wide range of regions and crops that reveal the negative impacts of climate change on crop yields and, consequently, on the livelihoods of those who rely on agriculture (IPCC 2014a: 6).

Flexibility and adaptability in the face of uncertainty are necessary for the poor who use agriculture as a primary source of income. In Mexico many small farmers rely on the production of maize as their principal source of income, notwithstanding the riskiness involved in this crop choice. Eakin (2005) conducted an ethnographic case study of three rural communities in central Mexico to evaluate the adaptive capacity of rural households dependent on maize production in the face of climatic changes. She concludes that, however risky, maize production serves as an insurance policy against the even greater risks of engaging in non-agrarian employment and migration.

---

[50]According to one standard reference, "Dry-land farming is made possible mainly by the fallow system of farming, a practice dating from ancient times. Basically, the term fallow refers to land that is plowed and tilled but left unseeded during a growing season. The practice of alternating wheat and fallow assumes that by clean cultivation the moisture received during the fallow period is stored for use during the crop season" (Encyclopedia Britannica 2014).

Climate change may also be having indirect and direct effects on both internal (rural-to- urban) and international migration. Cohen et al. (2013) highlight the dramatic impacts climate change has had on poor, rural livelihoods, where unstable climatic conditions have led to crop loss and food insecurity, making life based on agriculture unsustainable. Faced with such a threat to their livelihoods, rural dwellers have resorted increasingly to migration as a way to feed their families and generate some form of income (Cohen et al 2013). Barrios et al. (2006) make a similar claim with reference to sub-Saharan Africa, where climate change, especially in the form of increasing periods of drought, has led to large-scale, rural-to-urban migration. Another factor that may induce, or at least facilitate migration in response to negative climatic impacts is proximity to an international border (Cohen et al. 2013). In the case of Mexico, this implies that the increased impulse to migrate internationally may be somewhat restricted to those residing closer to the border with the United States.

While the literature on climate change, agriculture, and migration is not yet abundant, the works reviewed here do point to a tentative conclusion: climate change is increasing the uncertainty faced by those whose livelihood is tied to the land. In the sections that follow, we aim to document this increased uncertainty, and to analyze its consequences. We now turn to the results of our 2015 field study of Tunkás. In the following section, we analyze qualitative data gathered from interviews with Tunkaseños who have directly experienced the effects of climate change on agricultural production.

Impact of Climate Change on Agricultural Production in Tunkás

The following analysis is based on fifteen semi-structured interviews conducted in Tunkás during the months of January and February, 2015, supplemented by data from our standardized survey interviews in the town. Subjects for in-depth interviews were recruited based on their experience growing crops or practicing other forms of agriculture, primarily on communal land held as part of the town "ejido."[51]

Like other people of Mayan ancestry in southern Mexico, Tunkaseños have practiced agriculture, including the cultivation of corn, for many generations. Throughout the 20th Century, agriculture has been both an essential source of subsistence and a

---

[51] For a general description of changing land practices in rural Mexico, see Cornelius and Mhyre, eds. (1998).

lightning rod of conflict. In the aftermath of the Mexican Revolution of 1910-1920, a partial land reform conferred communal land rights upon the inhabitants of small towns like Tunkás. While many such places have privatized ejido landholdings in recent decades, Tunkás has maintained the institution of the ejido more or less unaltered. This means that Tunkaseños today continue to work plots of communal land allocated by a central body (the *comisariado ejidal*). In some cases, these communal plots are supplemented by private lands or grazing areas maintained by small groups of farmers.

Agriculture continues to be an important part of the economic livelihoods of Tunkaseños. Of the 415 unique households represented in our standardized survey, 143 (34 percent) reported having land currently in production in Tunkás. These Tunkaseños reported that working the land has become progressively more difficult over the space of a single generation. We asked them to identify the most important cause of increasing difficulty in agricultural production, and 50 percent attributed the increased difficulty to climate change.

Our semi-structured interviews allow us to identify the specific causal paths through which changes in climate are impacting the agricultural sector in Tunkás. We divide our discussion of these impacts into two sections. First we consider the impact that climate change has had on crop production, focusing on the greater prevalence of pests and the increasing salinization of agricultural land. We follow this with a discussion of the effects of changing temperature and precipitation on the local apiculture (bee-keeping) industry.

One of the key climate-change-related factors impacting the town's agriculture is the growing presence of agricultural pests. We found that farmers are losing crops during the growing season in part because of infestations of the *"langosta"* (locust). These grasshopper-like insects have been a threat to agricultural production all over the world. The locust consumes an amount of plant matter equivalent to its body mass, and in swarms of hundreds can be very destructive to vegetation (Showler 2013).[52] Researchers have found that with 15 millimeters of rain, locust eggs hatch almost instantaneously.

---

[52] In 1983-1984 researchers studying the effect of locusts on crops in the African nation of Mali found that these pests are more destructive during drought periods. When mid-summer rains were nonexistent and rains in October were inadequate, these conditions caused the locust to damage the crop early in the season as they hatched in swarms. In 1985, when rainfall returned to a state of "normality," the locust population declined (Jago 1987).

Later in the season more eggs are laid, but these enter a period of suspended development, hatching about six months later. Under drought conditions, eggs remain dormant until they come in contact with water, which leads to the simultaneous hatching of many insects, or a swarm (Jago 1987). According to Emmanuel, a Tunkaseño farmer, pests like the *langosta* are more common today than in the past and have become an important obstacle to successful crop yields:

> This growing season, there wasn't much rain. The *langosta* arrived and we were screwed. In November they started to hatch. They eat everything, and the corn plants yield nothing.

In response to the destruction wrought by these pests, many Tunkaseño farmers have adapted by using larger quantities of fertilizers and insecticides. According to Globally Important Agricultural Heritage Systems, the extensive use of fertilizers "has led to soil acidification, contamination of subsoil water, and increased production cost" (González 2002). At times when pests destroyed their vegetation entirely, farmers like Emmanuel have worked on other private and ejido plots, substituting crops grown there for their destroyed ones.

More generally, climate change-related drought has negatively impacted agricultural production in Tunkás. Of the Tunkaseños interviewed in our standardized survey who are currently working the land, 82.3 percent reported that they depend exclusively on the rain that falls to water their land or provide water for livestock, making them highly vulnerable to drought. Moreover, the terrain of the Yucatán Peninsula does not allow for proper drainage of chemicals that have accumulated from fertilizers and pesticides. Yucatán has a Karst landscape, meaning that it has soil containing limestone, dolomite, and gypsum. The Peninsula has an underground drainage system of *cenotes* (naturally occurring, mostly underground sinkholes that fill with water), but there is no way to pump that water to the surface.[53] As a result the surface becomes drier, and the water that comes from rainfall is contaminated by chemicals such as overused fertilizers.

In 2008, Tunkás experienced one of its driest growing seasons in many years, and numerous farmers lost most of their crops (Cornelius et al. 2010: 11). In our 2015

---

[53] The Yucatán typography is susceptible to salinization due to salt accumulation on the surface that results from a deep water table and poor drainage (Rengasamy, 2006; Sedov et al., 2008).

126

fieldwork we asked farmers how they viewed the effects of climatic conditions on their crops. A common response was that salty rainwater was making the leaves of plants yellow and red, ruining the harvest. As Jesús, a Tunkaseño farmer, put it: "The rain that falls is pure salt. It makes the plants die, and the harvest fails."

Our investigation identified two possible explanations for this phenomenon. First, misuse of pesticides and fertilizers could have increased the salinity of the topsoil. A study of traditional agricultural practices in Honduras found that indigenous beliefs, such as the view that all insects are harmful, trigger overuse of pesticides and fertilizers (Bentley 1989). These chemicals do produce an increase in yield for farmers, but their overuse has a variety of consequences, including damage to nutrients in soil, crop loss, pest resistance, and eutrophication, which is the excessive accumulation of nutrients in an ecosystem (Andersen & Pandya-Lorch, 1994; Chislock et al. 2013).

The second, possibly complementary, explanation for the so-called "salty" rain that now falls in Tunkás is that salt is stored in the soil due to inadequate drainage in the Yucateco landscape. The destruction of crops and the changing of color of the leaves could be due to the accumulation of salt from the terrain. When rainfall hits the surface, salt deposits may rise and destroy the crops.

In sum, climate change is interacting with the ecosystem of Tunkás to produce a variety of challenges for those households engaged in growing crops. These challenges have led Tunkaseño households to invest more intensively in their land, in an attempt to maintain adequate yield. As we shall now see, the town's apiculturists are facing similar problems, and responding in broadly similar ways.

Apiculture: The Flowers that Wilt

Apiculture has been an increasingly important source of income for families in the Yucatán Peninsula since the 1980s.[54] But in recent years this promising industry has been jeopardized by the effects of climate change, including a greater prevalence pests that destroy both the flora on which bees feed and the bees themselves. Climate change

---

[54] Bee-keeping in the Yucatan Peninsula began in pre-Columbian times, but it was not until the 1980s that honey production began to take off. The high quality of the honey produced in Yucatán made it an ideal product for export (Cornelius, et al. 2007: 13, 33-34).

has brought wider fluctuations in temperature and precipitation. Extreme heat (or cold) and lack of rain have taken a toll on the flora that bees need to produce honey. As Tunkaseño bee-keeper Humberto put it,

> When there is good weather, with heat and enough rain, the flowers bloom and there is a lot of nectar for the bees. This year the flowers bloomed, but with the extreme cold and heat they have withered. The flowers are very delicate, and with these conditions they just dry up. They don't produce nectar.

When the flowers wilt, the essential nutrients that bees obtain by drinking their nectar must be provided artificially. Many beekeepers in Tunkás have resorted to buying sugar and feeding it to their bees, a costly investment that reduces the total income of apiculturist families. Inadequate rainfall not only affects flower growth but also limits that amount of water that is available for bees to maintain their hives, further decreasing the output of honey.[55]

In addition, apiculturists have to invest in protecting their bees from pests that destroy the bees and eat any honey they have produced. Two specific pests that have affected honey production in Tunkás are *la varroa* and *el escarbajo*. These pests have not only affected apiculture in Mexico; *la varroa* is thought to be the most serious threat to the western bee.[56] A parasite that feeds on the bee, it can kill bee colonies within weeks.[57] The combination of *la varroa* and with other stressors on bees (like poor foraging weather related to climate change) makes the pest more lethal within bee colonies. Another pest, known among beekeepers in Tunkás as *el escarbajo* and among ecologists as *Aethina tumida,* feeds off the honey, wax, bee larvae, and even dead bees. Medications offer some protection from these pests, but *la varroa* has developed resistance to some

---

[55] Honey bees collect a variety of substances to ensure their survival. They collect nectar, which adult bees convert into honey and store in beeswax cells, and pollen, which provides most the protein, amino acids, fats, vitamins, and mineral requirements of a bee's diet. Bees also collect water, using it to maintain the temperature and humidity of the hive and to dilute stored honey for consumption (Somerville 2000).

[56] The *varroa* mite migrated from its original host, the Asian bee *Apis cerana*, to new host, *A. mellifera.*, which has spread to nearly all continents (VanEngelsdorp & Meixner 2010).

[57] Bees that have been infected by *la varroa* have shortened abdomens, misshapen wings, and other deformities. The young bees normally have short life spans.

treatments, and the medications are expensive. At some point, investing in drugs and other artificial means to maintain honey production in an era of climate change will become prohibitively expensive to the town's bee-keepers, and they are likely to consider alternative income-earning strategies, including migration.

IMPACTS OF CLIMATE CHANGE ON MIGRATION BEHAVIOR

Tunkáseños are constantly affected by climatic changes that threaten their standard of living. Not being able to live off their land as they previously did, increasingly they are seeking better-paying, non-agricultural employment. Already many have considered selling their labor elsewhere in Mexico or in the United States. We hypothesize that the increasing difficulty of agricultural production and migration are linked. The harder it gets to produce and make a profit from the land, the more likely it is that Tunkaseños will look for outside work. Furthermore, as the results above show, climate change has also made agriculture a more uncertain enterprise, and has forced Tunkaseño farmers to invest more of their time and money in raising crops or keeping bees.

In our quantitative analysis of data from our standardized survey of Tunkaseños, we constructed two different models of the decision to migrate as a function of climatic impacts on agriculture. The first model allows us to see the connection between agricultural uncertainty and international migration at the individual level. Our main independent variable of interest is a summative index which we created by aggregating responses to a series of questionnaire items that measured how difficult agriculture has become for people in Tunkás.[58] Specifically, the index combines information about changes in the amount of time and money the farmer invests in agriculture, the productivity of their fields or livestock produce, and the general difficulty involved in working the land. The index also includes information about whether the farmer is wholly dependent on rainfall, or has implemented some form of irrigation for their land. These questions asked about changes that have occurred since the interviewee began working the fields. The distribution of respondents on our summative index is reported in Figure 4.1. Higher scores on the index indicate greater perceived difficulty over time.

---

[58] Further details are provided in the appendix to this chapter.

129

Figure 4.1: Distribution of Interviewees on Summative Index of Increasing Difficulty in Agricultural Production

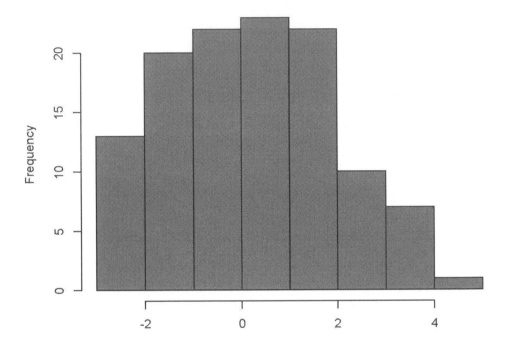

Among our interviewees currently working the land, 12 percent reported that the size of their landholdings had increased, while 9 percent said that it had decreased. The expanded landholdings of some respondents may be an adaptive response to climate change: Ejidatarios have been acquiring privately-held land to supplement diminished earnings from growing crops on their ejido plot. When asked how the time they spent working in their fields has changed since they began working the land, 28 percent indicated that time invested had increased, while 22 percent said they invested less time. More than one-third (35 percent) reported that they now invested more money in their fields, while 15 percent were investing less. Finally, when asked how the productivity of their fields has changed over time, 16 percent reported that they produce more, while 45 percent reported a drop in productivity. When our interviewees were asked if it was becoming more difficult to produce food for their family and make a profit from their fields, 80 percent responded that it was becoming more difficult while just 18 percent perceived no increase in difficulty.

The dependent variable in our first model is a summative index of "propensity to migrate to the United States." As explained in Chapter 1, this volume, the index aggregates the respondent's prior migration history (e.g., having ever migrated to the United States, the number of trips in the last five years), the total amount of time the respondent has spent in the United States (normalized to preserve scale), whether the respondent intends to migrate in the next 12 months, and whether or not the respondent is of prime migration age, which we define as being 18-35 years old. The index of increasing difficulty in agricultural production appears in the table as "Ag.more.diff". As additional controls, we include gender, age, highest level of educational attainment, and the number of relatives the respondent has who live in the United States.

As reported in Table 4.1, we found a positive relationship between our index of increased difficulty in agricultural production and propensity to migrate to the United States, significant at the alpha = 5% level (p = 0.063). The multivariate analysis shows that the most significant factors that determine a Tunkaseño's likelihood of migrating to the United States are gender and the number of relatives living in the United States.

Table 4.1: Multivariate Analysis: Predictors of Propensity to Migrate to the U.S.
(individual-level data; standard errors in parentheses)

Independent variables:	Dependent variable: Propensity to migrate to U.S.
Ag.more.diff	0.117*
	(0.063)
Gender: male	0.695***
	(0.262)
Age	-0.010
	(0.010)
Highest education	0.039
	(0.027)
# Relatives in U.S.	0.369***
	(0.057)
Constant	0.264
	(0.626)
Observations	110
R2	0.373
Adjusted R2	0.342
Residual Std. Error	1.193 (df=104)
F Statistic	12.351***
	(df=5;104)

Significance : *p<0.1; **p<0.05; ***p<0.01

The main conclusion of this analysis is that, insofar as climate change has made it more difficult for Tunkaseños to earn income from their lands, it is pushing them to explore international migration as an alternative. As agricultural production becomes less sustainable as a way of life, Tunkaseños must find other means of survival, and migration to the United States, which began in Tunkás in the 1970s, continues to be an important option.

Our second multivariate model uses household-level data to understand the relationship between pursuing agriculture as a form of generating income and the level of *internal* migration, i.e., to destinations with the Yucatán Peninsula or other regions of Mexico. For this analysis we split our sample into two groups: Tunkaseño households with land currently in production and those with no land in production. Table 4.2 reports descriptive statistics for these two groups. Overall, the two groups have similar socio-demographic characteristics, although members of households with land in production have significantly lower levels of educational attainment, and those having no land in production have stronger family ties to the United States.

Table 4.2: Descriptive Statistics for Tunkás Households, by Land in Production

	No land in production	Land in production
Age	40.3	42.8
Gender: male	0.38	0.42
Married: yes	0.63	0.69
Children: yes	0.75	0.80
# relatives in U.S.	1.37	1.07
Highest education	9.44*	7.81*
# of household possessions	4.60	5.17

*difference significant at the alpha = 1% level

For the regression analysis that follows, the main independent variable is whether the household has land in production. The main dependent variable, household-level internal migration, is constructed from a roster of household inhabitants reported by the first person interviewed in each dwelling. We asked these respondents to list the current place of residence of family members who had previously resided in the home. The resulting data allow us to estimate the incidence of internal migration among Tunkaseño households. For the present analysis, we construct a ratio with the number of former household members currently residing in other parts of Mexico as the numerator, and the total number of household members (current and former) as the denominator. As controls, we use the number of government social support programs in which one or

133

more members of the household participates, a count of durable consumer items possessed by the household, an indicator of whether the household receives remittances from members who have migrated, and a simple binary indicator of income sufficiency (is the income currently being received adequate to meet the household's needs).

Table 4.3: Multivariate Analysis: Predictors of Internal Migration
(household level data; standard errors in parentheses)

Independent variables:	Dependent variable:
	Household-level internal migration
Has land in production	-0.491*** (0.146)
Number of government programs benefitting household	-0.340*** (0.059)
Number of household possessions	0.065 (0.028)
Receives remittances	-0.375** (0.173)
Income sufficient to meet household needs: yes	0.262* (0.140)
Constant	-0.981*** (0.233)
Observations	306
Log Likelihood	-475.676
Akaike Inf. Crit.	963.352

Significance: $*p<0.1$; $**p<0.05$; $***p<0.01$

Table 4.3 reports the results of a binomial regression model with the dependent variable being the proportion of internal migrants in each household, as described above. The most interesting result of this analysis is the strongly negative relationship between having land in production and internal migration (the coefficient is significant at the alpha = 1% level). In other words, having land in production makes it less likely that families will pursue the option of internal migration.

Why would holding land that is actively worked make households less likely to depend on internal migration? Our answer, informed by the qualitative interviews referenced above, is that households with land in production view their land as an investment that requires continuous attention and maintenance. In households without active landholdings, it is easier for household members to explore employment and education options available in other parts of Mexico without being concerned that they will lose the value of the investments they have made in their land. These investments include medicines and other tools for protecting the health of bees, improvised irrigation systems, and access to local produce markets.

Of course it may be that another variable, not captured in our analysis, is leading to both a higher likelihood of landholding and lower rates of internal migration. While we cannot entirely discard this threat of omitted variable bias, the descriptive statistics in Table 4.2 suggest that, generally speaking, families with and without land in production are socio-demographically more similar than we might expect. Since the two groups of families are roughly equivalent in this sense, we posit that having land that is being worked exerts some causal effect on internal migration.

The best way to interpret the two sets of multivariate analysis results reported above is as follows. Looking at all households interviewed, we find that holding land leads to lower levels of *internal* migration. We explain this by pointing to the value of investments made in land, which require continued maintenance or else risk being lost. Separately, we focus on the subset of households with land currently in production. For this group of respondents, we find that the greater the impact of climate change on an individual's agricultural production, the higher their likelihood of *international* migration. Clearly, Tunkaseño families are using a complex mix of strategies to respond to a difficult and rapidly changing environment.

CONCLUSION

Members of a community whose economy is based largely on agricultural production, Tunkaseños have seen their livelihoods significantly affected by the recent increase in climate variability. Our qualitative interviews revealed that increases in heat, hard (or premature) frosts, and decreasing precipitation have caused crop losses while decimating the flora that beekeepers depend on for honey production. In addition, climate variability is encouraging voracious pests to descend upon the fields. Not surprisingly, Tunkaseños are looking for other means of generating income that are not dependent on agriculture.

Many have chosen the path of internal or international migration. As global warming continues and local climate changes become even more pronounced, the town will continue to see its residents leave town and find employment elsewhere. But migration is not an option – or at least an alternative perceived as feasible – for some Tunkaseños. As Pedro expressed it:

> I don't like working in the fields because it's work for slaves. When there is no production there is no money. My father wanted me and my brothers and sisters to get ahead, but now we lack the means. If we want to leave, say to the United States, just look at the problems one has there! If you don't know English, they don't give you work. And those of us who work in the fields don't have any chance to learn English. We don't know anything more than working the fields.

Thus, some Tunkaseños most likely will continue trying to extract a living from growing crops or producing honey, despite the much more challenging conditions created by climate change and the expensive new inputs that they must purchase to generate income from these activities. While changes in the local climate have become evident, their full effects have yet to be seen. It is possible that the combination of the youngest generation's disdain for laboring in the fields and greater variability in climate eventually could render obsolete the agricultural livelihood upon which Tunkaseños have depended for centuries.

REFERENCES CITED

Andersen, P., & Pandya-Lorch, R. (1994) Alleviating poverty, intensifying agriculture, and effectively managing natural resources. Discussion Paper , 2020 Vision Initiative, International Food Policy Research Institute, Washington, D.C.

Barrios, S. et al. (2006). Climate change and the rural-urban migration: The case of Sub-Saharan Africa. *Journal of Urban Economics,* 60 (3): 357-371.

Bentley, W., & Pandya-Lorch, R.J. (1989). What farmers don't know can't help them: The strengths and weaknesses of indigenous technical knowledge in Honduras. *Agriculture and Human Values,* 6(3): 25-31.

Chislock, M. , et al. (2013) Eutrophication: Causes, consequences, and controls in aquatic ecosystems. *Nature Education Knowledge* 4(4):10.

Cohen, S. et al. (2013). Forced migration, climate change mitigation and adaptive policies in Mexico: some functional relationships. *International Migration,* 51 (4): 53-72.

Cornelius, W., Fitzgerald, D., & Lewin-Fischer, P., eds. (2007). *Mayan Journeys: The New Migration from Yucatán to the United States.* La Jolla CA: Center for Comparative Immigration Studies, University of California-San Diego.

Cornelius W., Fitzgerald, D., Lewin-Fisher, P., & Muse-Orlinoff, L., eds. (2010) *Mexican Migration and the U.S. Economic Crisis.* La Jolla CA: Center for Comparative Immigration Studies, University of California-San Diego.

Cornelius, W., & Myhre, D., eds. (1998). *The Transformation of Rural Mexico: Reforming the Ejido Sector.* La Jolla CA: Center for U.S.-Mexican Studies, University of California-San Diego.

Eakin, H. (2005). Institutional change, climate risk, and rural vulnerability: cases from central Mexico. *World Development,* 33(11): 1923-38.

Encyclopedia Britannica (2014). "Agriculture." Retrieved from: http://www.merriam-webster.com/dictionary/agriculture.

González, C. (2002). "Milpa solar system: Mexico." Retrieved from: http://www.fao.org/giahs/giahs-sites/central-and-south-america/milpa-solar-system-mexico/detailed-information/en/

Gray, C.L. (2008). Environment, land, and rural out-Migration in the southern Ecuadorian Andes. *World Development,* 37 (2): 457-468.

IPCC (2014a). *Climate Change 2014: Impacts, Adaptation, and Vulnerability.* Cambridge, UK and New York: Cambridge University Press. "Summary for Policymakers, Part A: Global and Sectoral Aspects. Contribution of Working Group II to the Fifth Assessment Report of the Intergovernmental Panel on Climate Change."

IPCC (2014b). *Climate Change 2014: Mitigation of Climate Change.* Cambridge, UK and New York, NY: Cambridge University Press. "Contribution of Working Group III to the Fifth Assessment Report of the Intergovernmental Panel on Climate Change."

Jago, N. (1987) The return of the eighth plague. *New Scientist,* June 18.

Liverman, D. M., & O'Brien, K. L. (1991). Global warming and climate change in Mexico. *Global Environmental Change.* 1(5): 351-364.

Rengasamy, P. (2006). World salinization with emphasis on Australia. *Journal of Experimental Botany.* 57 (5): 1017-23.

Sedov, S., et al. (2008) Micromorphology of a soil catena in Yucatán: Pedogenesis and geomorphological processes in a tropical Karst landscape. Pp. 19-27 in Kapur, S., & Stoops, G., eds., *New Trends in Soil Micromorphology.* New York and Berlin: Springer-Verlag.

Showler, A. (2013) The desert locust in Africa and western Asia: Complexities of war, politics, perilous terrain, and development. In E. B. Radcliffe, W. D. Hutchison, & R. E. Cancelado, eds., *Radcliffe's IPM World Textbook.* St. Paul, MN: University of Minnesota. Retrieved from: http://ipmworld.umn.edu

Somerville. D. (July 2000). Honey bee nutrition and supplementary feeding. *NSW Agriculture,* Agnote ISSN 1034-6848, DAI/178, July. Retrieved from: http://dpi.nsw.gov.au

VanEnglesdorp, D., & Meixner, M. (2010). A historical review of managed honey bee populations in Europe and the United States and the factors that may affect them. *Journal of Invertebrate Pathology.* 103: 580-95.

APPENDIX

Components of Summative Index of Perceived Difficulty in Agricultural Production

Ahora, unas preguntas sobre los cambios que han habido en cuanto a sus terrenos desde que los empezó a trabajar.

163. Desde que empezó a trabajar estos terrenos, ¿cómo ha cambiado...?

		Más	Menos	Igual	NA	No sabe
a	El tamaño de sus terrenos	1	2	3	8888	9999
b	El tiempo que invierte en trabajar el campo (incluye tiempo de familia)	1	2	3	8888	9999
c	El dinero que invierte en el campo	1	2	3	8888	9999
d	La cantidad que produce cada hectárea	1	2	3	8888	9999

164. Por lo general, ¿diría usted que se está volviendo más difícil sacar comida y dinero de su campo?

166. ¿Usted depende exclusivamente de *la lluvia* para regar la cosecha?

The Mexican Migration Field Research and Training Program's fieldwork team in Tunkás, Yucatán, January-February 2015.

SELECCIÓN DEL ENTREVISTADO

¿Usted es Tunkaseño?

(si la persona dice NO, pregunte "¿De dónde es?" y "¿Y sus padres o abuelos?" Si ni la persona ni sus padres o abuelos son de Tunkás, agradécele su atención y busca otra persona)

(si la persona es joven:)   ¿Cuántos años tiene usted?

(Si la persona tiene entre 15 y 17 años, pida permiso del padre u otro adulto en la casa. Si el adulto le da permiso para hacer la entrevista, empiece. Si no, agradécele su atención.)

(si la persona es mayor:)   ¿En qué año nació usted?   _____

(si tiene menos de 15 años o más de 65 años [si nació la fecha de hoy o antes de esta fecha en 1949], pida hablar con otra persona)

1   Hace tres años, un grupo de estudiantes vino a Tunkás y al sur de California a realizar entrevistas. ¿Alguno de estos estudiantes lo entrevistó?

2   ¿Es esta casa/apartamento propiedad de usted o algún familiar, o rentada?

3   ¿Cuánto paga cada mes en renta o hipoteca?

4   Si tuviera la oportunidad de vender la casa donde vive, ¿cuánto cree que valdría?

5   ¿Alguien en este hogar tiene terrenos para agricultura en Tunkás?

6   ¿Sabe usted el valor de estos terrenos?

7   ¿Quién los trabaja? (LEA CADA OPCIÓN E INDIQUE SÍ O NO.)

		Sí	No	NA	NS/NQR
a	Usted	1	2	8888	9999
b	Su pariente	1	2	8888	9999
c	Peón o empleado	1	2	8888	9999
d	Otra persona	1	2	8888	9999
e	Nadie	1	2	8888	9999

8   ¿Para qué se usan los terrenos?
     (LEA CADA OPCIÓN E INDIQUE SÍ O NO.)

		Sí	No	NA	NS/NQR
a	Milpa / Siembra para la familia (maíz)	1	2	8888	9999
b	Milpa / Siembra para vender (maíz)	1	2	8888	9999
c	Otra siembra para la familia Especifique _____	1	2	8888	9999
d	Otra siembra para vender Especifique _____	1	2	8888	9999
e	Ganadería para la familia	1	2	8888	9999
f	Ganadería para vender animales	1	2	8888	9999
g	Apicultura	1	2	8888	9999
h	Otro	1	2	8888	9999
i	Terrenos no en producción	1	2	8888	9999

9   Pedir detalles sobre la extensión de los terrenos y la ganadería:

		Nº	NA	NS/NQR
a	Nº de colmenas		8888	9999
b	Nº de cabezas de ganado		8888	9999
c	Nº de hectáreas		8888	9999
d	(Si no sabe el número de hectáreas) Nº de mecates		8888	9999

10   ¿Considera usted que el ingreso actual de la casa alcanza para los gastos de la vida cotidiana (comida, renta, ropa, mantener a su familia)?

11   Pensando en el primer mes del año escolar en curso, ¿cuánto se tuvo que gastar para la escuela? (Esto incluye colegiatura, uniformes, útiles, y transporte.)

> ➢ **PREGUNTE SÓLO AL PRIMER ADULTO ENCUESTADO EN LA CASA QUE VIVE EN MÉXICO.**
>
> ➢ **SI NO VIVE EN MÉXICO, PASE A # 26.**

---

12   ¿Alguien en su casa tiene Seguro Popular?

13   ¿Alguien en su casa participa en el programa PROCAMPO (Programa de Apoyos Directos al Campo)?

14   ¿Alguien en su casa participa en el programa PROGAN (Programa de Producción Pecuaria Sustentable y Ordenamiento Ganadero y Apícola)?

15   ¿Alguien en su hogar recibe algún beneficio de otro programa de apoyo del gobierno? (Por ejemplo, Prospera (antes Oportunidades), ProÁrbol, Vivienda Digna, PROCAPI (Programa de Coordinación Para el Apoyo a la Productividad Indígena), MCRNZI (Proyecto de Manejo y Conservación de Recursos Naturales en Zonas Indígenas), POPMI (Programa de Organización Productiva para Mujeres Indígenas), PROIN (Programa para Mejoramiento de la Producción y la Productividad Indígena), PROI (Programa de Infraestructura Indígena).

16   ¿De qué material es la mayor parte del piso de la casa donde usted vive?

17   ¿De qué material es la mayor parte del techo de la casa donde Ud. vive?

18   ¿En este hogar alguien tiene…?
      (LEA CADA OPCIÓN E INDIQUE SÍ O NO.)

	Artículo	Sí	No	NA	NS/NQR
a	Automóvil, camioneta o moto	1	2	8888	9999
b	Tractor	1	2	8888	9999
c	Televisión	1	2	8888	9999
d	DVD (reproductor)	1	2	8888	9999
e	Computadora personal	1	2	8888	9999
f	Internet	1	2	8888	9999
g	Refrigerador	1	2	8888	9999
h	Estufa de gas o parrilla eléctrica	1	2	8888	9999
i	Horno de microondas	1	2	8888	9999
j	Lavadora automática para ropa	1	2	8888	9999
k	Secadora para ropa	1	2	8888	9999
l	Calentador para agua (boiler)	1	2	8888	9999
m	Tinaco	1	2	8888	9999

19   ¿Algún miembro de su hogar cultiva hortalizas en el solar?

20   ¿Tienen animales de traspatio o colmenas?

21   ¿Alguien en su hogar recibe dinero de alguien en los EEUU?

22   ¿En promedio cuánto dinero reciben en un mes típico?

23   De la cantidad que reciben, ¿se usa una parte para gastos escolares?
24   De ese dinero que reciben, ¿alguna parte se invierte en el campo?

25   ¿Alguien en su casa tiene alguna propiedad a su nombre en los EEUU (incluye
      casa, condominio, terrenos)?

> ➤ PREGUNTE AL PRIMER ADULTO ENCUESTADO QUE VIVE EN LOS EEUU.
>
> ➤ SI NO VIVE EN LOS EEUU, PASE A # 28.

27   ¿Cuántas personas dependen de este ingreso (incluye las personas en
      México a quienes se les envían remesas)?

> ➤ PREGUNTE AL PRIMER ADULTO ENCUESTADO.

28   Ahora vamos a hablar de la gente de su familia que ha vivido en su casa en los
      últimos dos meses o alguna vez ha vivido en su casa y se fue a otro lugar
      (incluye padres, parejas, hijos, sobrinos, hermanos, etc.). Pensando en todas
      estas personas, ¿me podría decir los datos siguientes? (Empiece con el/la
      entrevistado/a.):

      Parentesco con Ud.?
      Dónde nació?
      Dónde vive actualmente, o dónde murió?
      Nivel más alto de educación?
      Actualmente está estudiando?

> ➢ PREGUNTE A TODOS.

INFORMACIÓN DEMOGRÁFICA

29   ¿En qué año nació usted?

30   Anote el sexo de la persona.

31   ¿Dónde nació usted?

32   ¿Dónde vive usted actualmente la mayor parte del tiempo?

33   ¿Usted piensa regresar a México este año, de manera *permanente?*

34   ¿Por qué piensa regresar?

35   Y de las razones que Ud. mencionó (en la pregunta anterior), ¿cuál es la razón
      más importante?

36   En los últimos 5 años, ¿dónde ha pasado más tiempo, en Tunkás, otra localidad
      en México o en los EEUU?

37   En los últimos 5 años, ¿ha viajado fuera de los EEUU en algún
      momento?

38   ¿Estuvo en los EEUU el 20 de noviembre 2014?

39   ¿Asiste usted actualmente a la escuela?

40   ¿Alguna vez asistió a la escuela?

41   ¿En qué nivel empezó la escuela, y hasta qué nivel aprobó? ¿Y dónde estudió –
      en México o los Estados Unidos?

> ➢ PREGUNTE A LOS QUE ACTUALMENTE SON ESTUDIANTES.

> ➢ SI NO ES ESTUDIANTE, PASE A # 45.

---

42   ¿Qué nivel escolar le gustaría terminar?
      (USAR LOS CÓDIGOS EN EL CUADRO DE EDUCACIÓN.)

43   ¿Qué nivel escolar piensa que <u>es posible</u> terminar?

44   ¿Qué nivel piensa que sus padres quisieran que usted complete? (

45   ¿En qué nivel empezó la escuela, y hasta qué nivel aprobó <u>su padre</u>? ¿Y dónde
        estudió – en México o en los Estados Unidos?

46   ¿En qué nivel empezó la escuela, y hasta qué nivel aprobó <u>su madre</u>? ¿Y dónde
        estudió?

47   ¿Puede usted leer, hablar, entender y escribir inglés? – bien, poco, o nada? ¿Y
        en español – bien, poco, o nada? ¿Y en maya – bien, poco. O nada?

48   ¿Usted practica alguna religión? Cuál?

49   ¿Qué tan seguido va a misa/al servicio religioso?

50   ¿Pertenece usted a alguno de los siguientes grupos?
        (LEA LAS OPCIONES. MARQUE TODAS LAS QUE APLIQUEN.)

                1 Un grupo jaranero
                2 Un equipo de deporte no profesional
                3 Un gremio
                4 Un grupo religioso
                5 Otro tipo de grupo

Cuadro de educación

México	Nivel en México	Nivel en EEUU	EEUU
0	Preescolar y Kinder	Preschool y Kindergarten	0
1	1º de primaria	1º grado	1
2	2º de primaria	2º grado	2
3	3º de primaria	3º grado	3
4	4º de primaria	4º grado	4
5	5º de primaria	5º grado	5
6	6º de primaria	6º grado	6
7	1º de secundaria*	7º grado	7
8	2º de secundaria *	8º grado	8
9	3º de secundaria*	9º grado	9
		Entrenamiento técnico	10
11	1º de preparatoria **	10º grado	11
12	2º de preparatoria **	11º grado	12
13	3º de preparatoria **	12º grado	13
14	1º de universidad ***	1º de universidad †	14
15	2º de universidad ***	2º de universidad †	15
16	3º de universidad ***	3º de universidad †	16
17	4º de universidad ***	4º de universidad †	17
18	5º de universidad ***	1º de estudios posgrados ††	18
19	1º de estudios posgrados****	2º de estudios posgrados ††	19
20	2º de estudios posgrados****	3º de estudios posgrados ††	20
21	3º de estudios posgrados****	4º de estudios posgrados ††	21
22	4º de estudios posgrados****	5º de estudios posgrados ††	22

* Telesecundaria, secundaria general, secundaria técnica, etc.

** CONALEP, bachillerato, CBTA (Centro de Bachillerato Tecnológico Agropecuario), Media Superior etc.

*** Licenciatura, normal, carrera, etc.

**** Maestría, doctorado etc.

† Associate's Degree, BA, BS, etc.

†† Master's, PhD, MD, JD, etc.

51   ¿Cuál es su estado civil?

52   ¿Dónde vive su pareja?

53   Ahora le voy a preguntar acerca de otros miembros de su **familia** (no importa donde viven).

Pariente	Total		¿Cuántos viven en Tunkás?	¿Cuántos viven en EEUU?	¿Cuántos viven en otras partes de México?
Hermanos/hermanas y hermanitos/hermanitas	a	b		c	d
Padres	e	f		g	h
Abuelos y abuelas	i	j		k	l

Ahora le voy a preguntar algunos datos sobre los hijos e hijas que usted ha tenido.

54   ¿Cuántos hijos tiene Ud.?

> ➤ PREGUNTE A LOS QUE TIENEN HIJOS.
> ➤ SI NO TIENE HIJOS, PASE A # 56.

55   Empezando con su hijo mayor, ¿me podría decir en qué año y país nació cada uno de sus hijos, y donde vive actualmente?

        (Si vive en los Estados Unidos:)
        Cuál es su estatus migratorio?

> ➤ PREGUNTE A TODOS.

56   ¿A qué se dedica Ud. principalmente?

57   ¿Cuál es su puesto en el trabajo?

58   ¿En total, cuántas horas trabaja en una semana típica?

59   En comparación con el año pasado, ¿trabaja más horas por semana, menos horas por semana o es igual?

60   ¿En promedio cuánto gana en un mes típico?

61   ¿En el último año, pasó algo que haya afectado a su familia económicamente?

148

(Si la persona vive en México, lea estos ejemplos:) Por ejemplo, perdió su cosecha, problemas con el ganado, fracaso de negocio, enfermedad familiar, deportación.

(Si la persona vive en los EEUU, lea estos ejemplos:) Por ejemplo, pérdida de trabajo, menos horas en el trabajo, fracaso de negocio, enfermedad familiar.

62   ¿Después de este evento, realizó alguna de las siguientes actividades para cubrir sus gastos de la vida cotidiana? (LEA LAS OPCIONES Y MARQUE TODAS LAS QUE APLIQUEN.)

> 1 Empleo informal (vender comida, vender ropa)
> 2 Vender terrenos o animales
> 3 Buscar trabajo en los EEUU u otro lugar en México
> 4 Pedir prestado al banco
> 5 Pedir prestado a parientes y/o amigos
> 6 Otro

63   ¿Usted diría que en general su salud es...(LEA LAS OPCIONES.)

> 1 excelente?
> 2 muy buena?
> 3 buena?
> 4 más o menos?
> 5 mala?

64   ¿Tiene algún problema médico que requiere atención médica frecuente?

65   ¿Dónde se le facilita más recibir atención médica para este problema? (LEA LAS OPCIONES.)

> 1 Yucatán
> 2 Estados Unidos
> 3 Otra parte de México

HISTORIA MIGRATORIA

66   ¿Es usted ciudadano de los Estados Unidos?

67   ¿En qué año recibió la ciudadanía?

68   ¿Tiene usted green card o residencia legal permanente en los EEUU?

69   ¿En qué año recibió su green card?

70   ¿Actualmente usted tiene algo que le permite residir en los Estados Unidos temporalmente (Por ejemplo, como visa de estudiante, visa de turista, DACA u otra suspensión de deportación)?

➤ PREGUNTE A TODOS QUE NACIERON EN MÉXICO.
➤ SI NACIÓ EN LOS EEUU, PASE A LA SECCION DE <u>MIGRACIÓN</u> (# 130).

Viaje	¿A dónde fue?	¿En qué año llegó?	¿Cuánto tiempo duró este viaje? (meses)	¿En qué trabajó/trabajaba?	¿Cuál fue/era su puesto en el trabajo?
Primer					
Último					

71   ¿Alguna vez ha salido de Tunkás para vivir o trabajar en otra parte de México?

Códigos: Lugar de destino
1 Cancún
2 Playa del Carmen
3 Mérida
4 Otra parte de la Península de Yucatán
5 Otra parte de México

Códigos: Ocupación
1 Estudiante/menor
2 Ama de casa
3 Jubilado
4 Otro económicamente inactivo (no busca trabajo)
5 Desempleado (busca trabajo)
6 Construcción y oficios relacionados
7 Agricultura/ Ganadería/Apicultura
8 Servicio (no profesional) (ejemplos: hotel, limpieza, conserje—excluye restaurante)
9 Servicio (profesional) (ejemplos: abogado, médico, maestro, mecánico)
10 Restaurante
11 Industria (manufactura)
12 Negocio o comercio propio
13 Otro económicamente activo

Códigos: Puesto en el trabajo
1 Patrón (**alguien que tiene empleados**. e.j.: ejidatario/a que contrata, dueño de un negocio, socio de unidad ganadera)
2 Trabajador por su cuenta (**no tiene empleados** e.j., ejidatario/a que trabaja su propio terreno, dueño de un pequeño negocio)
3 Trabajador a **sueldo fijo**, salario (trabaja para otra persona o una empresa regularmente)
4 Jornalero (trabaja por día y ocasionalmente)
5 Trabajador por pieza o comisión (venta de catálogo)
6 Trabajador sin pago

150

73   (En caso de "sí") Hablando de la última vez en que hizo esto...

¿A dónde iba?	¿En qué año empezó?	¿Cuánto tiempo duró el trabajo? (meses)	¿En qué trabajó/trabajaba?	¿Cuál fue/era su puesto en el trabajo?

Códigos: Lugar de destino
1 Cancún
2 Playa del Carmen
3 Mérida
4 Otra parte de la Península de Yucatán
5 Otra parte de México
8888 NA
9999 NS/NQR

Códigos: Ocupación
1 Estudiante/menor
2 Ama de casa
3 Jubilado
4 Otro económicamente inactivo (no busca trabajo)
5 Desempleado (busca trabajo)
6 Construcción y oficios relacionados
7 Agricultura/ Ganadería/Apicultura
8 Servicio (no profesional) (ejemplos: hotel, limpieza, conserje—excluye restaurante)
9 Servicio (profesional) (ejemplos: abogado, médico, maestro, mecánico)
10 Restaurante
11 Industria (manufactura)
12 Negocio o comercio propio
13 Otro económicamente activo
8888 NA

9999 NS/NQR

Códigos: Puesto en el trabajo
1 Patrón (**alguien que tiene empleados**. e.j.: ejidatario/a que contrata, dueño de un negocio, socio de unidad ganadera)
2 Trabajador por su cuenta (**no tiene empleados** e.j., ejidatario/a que trabaja su propio terreno, dueño de un pequeño negocio)
3 Trabajador a **sueldo fijo**, salario (trabaja para otra persona o una empresa regularmente)
4 Jornalero (trabaja por día y ocasionalmente)
5 Trabajador por pieza o comisión (venta de catálogo)
6 Trabajador sin pago
8888 NA
9999 NS/NQR

74   La última vez que usted se fue a otra parte de México, ¿por qué decidió irse a otra parte de México, en lugar de los Estados Unidos?

75   ¿ Y de las razones que Ud. mencionó (en la pregunta anterior), ¿cuál es la razón *más importante* en su decisión de irse a otra parte de México en lugar de los Estados Unidos?

76   ¿Alguna vez ha intentado ir a los EEUU, para vivir o trabajar?

77   *(En caso de "no":)* ¿Por qué ha decidido quedarse en México?

78   Y de las razones que Ud. mencionó (en la pregunta anterior), ¿cuál es la razón *más importante* en su decisión de quedarse en México?

CUADRO DE MIGRACION INTERNACIONAL

(Preguntar sobre cada viaje a los EEUU, desde el primer hasta el último viaje:)

¿A dónde iba? (lugar de destino: ciudad y estado)
¿En qué ano llegó o intentó cruzar?
¿Cuáles documentos usó?
¿Cuántas veces intentó cruzar?
¿Pudo cruzar?
¿Usó pollero?
¿Cuánto pagó al pollero, en dólares?
¿Cuánto tiempo duró este viaje en EEUU, en meses?

79   *(Pregunte a los que viven actualmente en México y han vivido en EEUU)*
¿Por qué regresó a vivir a México?

80   Y de las razones que Ud. mencionó (en la pregunta anterior), ¿cuál era
la razón *más importante*?

(SI TODAVÍA VIVE EN LOS EEUU O NUNCA PUDO ENTRAR A LOS EEUU:)

Ahora quisiera preguntarle sobre su ÚLTIMO viaje a los Estados Unidos, o su ÚLTIMO
intento de cruzar la frontera.

81   Hay muchas razones por las que la gente se va a los Estados Unidos. ¿Cuáles
fueron las razones más importantes para usted, la última vez que se fue?

82   Y de las razones que Ud. mencionó (en la pregunta anterior), ¿cuál era la razón
más importante para usted la última vez que se fue?

83   Cuando usted se fue a los EEUU, esta última vez, ¿tuvo que dejar a sus hijos en
México?

84   *(En caso de "sí")* ¿Quién los cuidó?

85   Si usó pollero, ¿en dónde conoció al pollero que le ayudó a cruzar?

86   ¿Quién se lo recomendó?

87   ¿El pollero cumplió con lo acordado?

88   ¿Cómo trató de pasar por la frontera?

       1 Por un aeropuerto en avión
       2 Por una garita (a pie o en vehículo)
       3 A pie por otra parte (incluye caminando por el desierto o la montaña)
       4 Nadando
       5 En barco o lancha
       6 Por un túnel subterráneo

89   ¿Durante su último viaje a la frontera, le ocurrió alguna de las siguientes
      situaciones? (LEA CADA OPCIÓN. MARQUE TODAS LAS QUE APLIQUEN.)

	Tipo de violencia	Sí	No	NA	NS /NQR	(Si respondió sí:) ¿Sabe quién lo hizo? (Usar códigos)
a	Lo/la asaltaron	1	2	8888	9999	
b	Lo/la golpearon	1	2	8888	9999	
c	Abusaron de usted	1	2	8888	9999	
d	Lo/la extorsionaron	1	2	8888	9999	
e	Lo/la secuestraron	1	2	8888	9999	

Códigos: Agresor
1 Patrulla fronteriza
2 Policía mexicana
3 Crimen organizado
4 Rateros
5 Pollero
6 Otro

90   ¿Cuántas veces fue agarrado/detenido en este último intento?

91   *(En caso de ser detenido:)* ¿Cuánto tiempo estuvo preso?

92   Al final, ¿pudo pasar o no?

93   *(En caso de "no":)* Después de no poder cruzar, ¿qué pasó?

        1 Regresó a Tunkás
        2 Regresó a otra parte de México (no en la frontera)
        3 Se quedó a vivir o trabajar en la frontera (en México)
        4 Otro
94   ¿Dónde vivía o trabajaba?

95   ¿Cuánto tiempo estuvo en este lugar?

➢ **PREGUNTE A LOS QUE ALGUNA VEZ PUDIERON ENTRAR A LOS E QUE VIVEN ACTUALMENTE EN MÉXICO. SI TODAVÍA SE ENCUENT LOS EEUU, PASE A # 100.**

➢ **SI NUNCA PUDO ENTRAR A LOS EEUU, PASE A # 118.**

---

96   Pensando en la última vez que estuvo en los EEUU, ¿a qué se dedicó
        principalmente?

97   ¿Cuál era su puesto en el trabajo?

98   ¿En total, cuántas horas trabajaba por semana?

99   ¿En promedio cuánto ganaba en este trabajo en un mes típico?

100   ¿Cómo consiguió su último trabajo en los EEUU?

        1 Regresó a un empleo anterior
        2 Parientes lo recomendaron al patrón
        3 Amigos o vecinos lo recomendaron al patrón
        4 Hablando directamente con el patrón
        5 Una agencia
        6 Buscando en la calle
        7 Periódico o radio
        8 No trabaja
        9 Otro

101   ¿Cómo cuánto tiempo necesitó para conseguir ese trabajo?

102   ¿Qué tan difícil fue encontrar trabajo en su último viaje a los Estados
        – muy difícil, algo difícil, poco difícil, o nada difícil?

Ahora quiero preguntarle más sobre sus experiencias en los EEUU en cualquier
momento—no importa si fue su último viaje a los EEUU o no.

103   ¿Alguna vez lo/la ha parado la policía en los EEUU?

104   *(En caso de "sí":)* ¿Qué le pasó después del encuentro con la policía?
        (LEA LAS OPCIONES.)

	Respuesta	Sí	No	NA	NS/NQR
a	Lo detuvieron unas horas	1	2	8888	9999
b	Lo encarcelaron más de un día	1	2	8888	9999
c	Le pusieron una multa	1	2	8888	9999
d	Le quitaron el carro	1	2	8888	9999
e	Lo reportaron a la migra	1	2	8888	9999
f	Nada pasó	1	2	8888	9999
g	Otro	1	2	8888	9999

105   ¿Tiene usted una orden de deportación pendiente?

106   ¿Ha sido usted deportado alguna vez?

107   *(En caso de "sí":)* Hablando de la última vez que le deportaron, ¿en qué año ocurrió?

108   ¿Y, en dónde le detuvieron? (LEA LAS OPCIONES.)

       1 En la frontera
       2 En la interior del país

109   ¿Cuánto tiempo estuvo preso?

110   ¿Buscó ayuda legal?

111   *(En caso de "sí":)* ¿De quién?

112   ¿Lo llevaron ante un juez?

113   ¿Le dieron la oportunidad de regresar a México luego luego después de haber firmado un papel? (lo que se llama, "repatriación voluntaria")

114   ¿Le dieron una orden que le prohíbe entrar a los EEUU después de su deportación?

115   *(En caso de "sí":)* ¿Por cuántos años le prohibieron entrar a los EEUU?

116   ¿Aun así, piensa usted regresar a los EEUU?

117   *(En caso de "sí":)* ¿Cuándo piensa regresar a los EEUU?

118   ¿Sus familiares, amigos o conocidos que viven en los EEUU le han dicho que han sufrido por falta de trabajo o menos horas de trabajo en los últimos 12 meses?

119   Desde el 2012, ¿alguien en su casa ha regresado de los EEUU a Tunkás por falta de trabajo?

120   ¿Piensa usted irse a vivir o trabajar en alguna otra parte de Yucatán o de México este año 2015?

121   *(En caso de "sí":)* ¿A dónde?

122   ¿Piensa ir a los EEUU para vivir o trabajar este año 2015?

123   *(En caso de "sí":)* ¿A dónde?

124   ¿Piensa cruzar con un pollero?

125   *(En caso de "sí":)* ¿Cómo piensa contratar al pollero?

       1 Amigos en los EEUU
       2 Familiares en los EEUU
       3 Cerca de la frontera
       4 Amigos en Tunkás
       5 Familiares en Tunkás
       6 Otro (especifique) _____

126   ¿Cuánto piensa que le costaría contratar un pollero?

127   ¿Por qué NO piensa ir a los EEUU este año para vivir o trabajar?

128   De las razones que Ud. mencionó (en la pregunta anterior), ¿cuál es la razón *más importante?*

129   Si usted pudiera cruzar la frontera gratis y sin peligro, ¿iría a los EEUU para vivir o trabajar este año 2015?

EXPERIENCIAS DE MIGRACIÓN

Ahora voy a preguntarle sobre sus opiniones acerca de la experiencia de cruzar la frontera.

130   De las cosas en estos dibujos, ¿cuáles son las tres cosas que más le preocupan a una persona que va a cruzar la frontera?

       (MUESTRE DIBUJOS Y ANOTE EL ORDEN DE LAS RESPUESTAS.)

	1ª Respuesta	2ª respuesta	3ª respuesta
Ser secuestrado	1	1	1
Ser asaltado	2	2	2
Ser encarcelado	3	3	3
La migra	4	4	4
El muro	5	5	5
Clima extremo	6	6	6
NA	8888	8888	8888
NS/NQR	9999	9999	9999

131   Actualmente, ¿qué tan difícil es cruzar la frontera sin papeles sin ser detenido? (LEA LAS OPCIONES.)

        1 Muy difícil
        2 Algo difícil
        3 Poco difícil
        4 Nada difícil

132   Hace 5 años, ¿qué tan difícil era cruzar la frontera sin ser detenido? (LEA LAS OPCIONES.)

        1 Muy difícil
        2 Algo difícil
        3 Poco difícil
        4 Nada difícil

133   Actualmente, ¿qué tan peligroso es cruzar la frontera, si uno no tiene papeles? (LEA LAS OPCIONES.)

        1 Muy peligroso
        2 Algo peligroso
        3 Poco peligroso
        4 Nada peligroso

134   *Hace 5 años*, si uno no tenía papeles, ¿qué tan peligroso era cruzar la frontera sin papeles? (LEA LAS OPCIONES.)

　　　　1 Muy peligroso
　　　　2 Algo peligroso
　　　　3 Poco peligroso
　　　　4 Nada peligroso

135   ¿Conoce personalmente a alguien que se fue a los EEUU y que murió al cruzar la frontera?

136   ¿Conoce a alguien que fue secuestrado al cruzar la frontera?

137   Algunas personas creen que ya es peligroso contratar un coyote porque puede estar trabajando con el crimen organizado. Otros piensan que no es peligroso porque los coyotes todavia trabajan por su cuenta. ¿Que piensa Ud?

Ahora quisiera preguntarle sobre sus opiniones acerca de encontrar empleo. Pensando en todo *la Península de Yucatán*, es decir los estados de Yucatán, Campeche y Quintana Roo…

139   ¿Qué tan fácil o difícil diría usted que era encontrar empleo en la Península de Yucatán, hace 5 años? (LEA LAS OPCIONES.)

　　　　1 Muy fácil
　　　　2 Algo fácil
　　　　3 Algo difícil
　　　　4 Muy difícil

140   ¿Qué tan fácil o difícil diría usted que es encontrar empleo en la Península de Yucatán, actualmente? (LEA LAS OPCIONES.)

　　　　1 Muy fácil
　　　　2 Algo fácil
　　　　3 Algo difícil
　　　　4 Muy difícil

141   ¿Qué tan factible sería conseguir un trabajo en Tunkás que le pagara dos salarios mínimos? (LEA LAS OPCIONES.)

　　　　1 Muy factible
　　　　2 Algo factible
　　　　3 Nada factible (o no hay trabajo en Tunkás)

142   ¿Qué tan factible sería conseguir un trabajo en otra parte de la Península de Yucatán que le pagara dos salarios mínimos? (LEA LAS OPCIONES.)

　　　　1 Muy factible
　　　　2 Algo factible
　　　　3 Nada factible (o no hay trabajo en la Península de Yucatán)

Ahora pensando en *los Estados Unidos*…

143   ¿Qué tan fácil o difícil es encontrar un trabajo en los EEUU, *actualmente*? (LEA
        LAS OPCIONES.)

        1 Muy fácil
        2 Algo fácil
        3 Algo difícil
        4 Muy difícil

144   *Hace 5 años,* ¿qué tan fácil o difícil era encontrar un trabajo en los
        EEUU? (LEA LAS OPCIONES.)

        1 Muy fácil
        2 Algo fácil
        3 Algo difícil
        4 Muy difícil

145   Algunas personas dicen que los que nacieron en Tunkás pueden progresar en
        la vida sin salir del pueblo. Otras personas dicen que para superarse, la gente de
        Tunkás tienen que ir a otro lugar. ¿Qué diría usted? (LEA ALTERNATIVAS.)

        1 Pueden superarse sin salir
        2 Tienen que salir

146   ¿Me podría decir si en los últimos cinco años, las deportaciones de mexicanos
        han aumentado, bajado, o se han quedado igual?

147   ¿Tiene usted algún familiar o amigo cercano que haya sido deportado
        en los últimos 5 años?

148   *(En caso de "sí":)* ¿Tiene esta persona una orden del gobierno que le
        prohíbe entrar a los EEUU tras su deportación?

149   ¿Conoce usted el programa del gobierno estadounidense que impide que los
        jóvenes migrantes sean deportados? El programa se llama "Suspensión de
        Deportación para los Llegados en la Infancia," que también se conoce como
        DACA.

150   *(En caso de "sí":)* De lo que usted sepa, ¿qué es lo que recibe un individuo que
        califica para este programa? (NO LEA LAS OPCIONES. MARQUE TODAS LAS
        QUE APLIQUEN.)

        1 Autorización para trabajar
        2 Permiso de tres años de residencia legal
        3 Número de seguro social
        4 Posibilidad de sacar permiso de conducir
        5 Camino a la ciudadanía
        6 Residencia permanente (green card)
        7 Beneficios del gobierno
        8 Posibilidad de traer a sus familiares a los EEUU
        9 No mencionó ninguno

151   ¿Cómo se enteró del programa DACA?

        1 Un amigo

2 Un pariente
3 El personal de la escuela/universidad
4 Una organización sin fines de lucro
5 El consulado
6 La televisión/radio
6 Otro

> ➢ PREGUNTE SÓLO A LAS PERSONAS QUE VIVEN EN LOS EEUU.

---

152 ¿Ha hecho una solicitud para DACA?

153 *(En caso de "sí":)* ¿Su solicitud de DACA ha sido aprobada, negada o está pendiente?

154 *(En caso de "no":)* ¿Piensa usted hacer una solicitud para DACA?

155 *(En caso de "no":)* ¿Por qué piensa no aplicar para DACA?
    (NO LEA OPCIONES. MARQUE TODAS LAS QUE APLIQUEN.)

    1 No necesito DACA porque soy ciudadano, residente permanente o tengo una visa.
    2 Creo que no califico para DACA (No cumplo con todos los requisitos.)
    3 No tengo dinero para solicitar DACA
    4 No sé cómo aplicar para DACA (necesita ayuda)
    5 No puedo proveer la documentación requerida para solicitar DACA
    6 Ya estoy empleado. No necesito autorización para trabajar
    7 DACA no ofrece suficientes beneficios (es temporal, no ofrece camino a la ciudadanía/residencia permanente)
    8 Tengo miedo que si yo someto una solicitud, puede poner a mí o a mi familia en peligro de ser deportado
    9 Otro

> ➢ PREGUNTE A TODOS.

---

156 Hace poco, el Presidente Obama tomó algunas acciones para que más de los indocumentados puedan quedarse en los Estados Unidos, sin temor de ser deportados. ¿Ud. ha oído hablar de estas acciones del Presidente Obama?

> ➢ PREGUNTE SÓLO A LAS PERSONAS QUE VIVEN EN LOS EEUU.

---

157 Para recibir la suspensión de deportación por este programa, una persona viviendo en los EEUU sin documentos tiene que cumplir con varios requisitos. Hay que:

1. Ser padre de un ciudadano estadounidense o un residente permanente legal.
2. Haber vivido continuamente en los EEUU desde el 1 de enero de 2010.
3. Haber estado en los Estados Unidos el 20 de noviembre de 2014.
4. Someterse a una revisión de antecedentes penales.

Pensando en estos requisitos, ¿piensa usted que cumple con los requisitos de este programa?

158   ¿Qué requisito no puede cumplir?
       (MARQUE TODAS LAS QUE APLIQUEN.)

       1 No tengo un hijo que es ciudadano o es residente permanente legal
       2 No he vivido en los EEUU continuamente desde el 1 de enero 2010
       3 No estuve en los EEUU el 20 de noviembre de 2014
       4 Tengo antecedentes penales

159   ¿Piensa usted hacer una solicitud para una suspensión de deportación?

MIGRACIÓN Y MEDIO AMBIENTE

160   ¿Es usted **ejidatario/a** en Tunkás?

161   ¿Usted decide cómo se usan los terrenos en Tunkás que pertenecen a su familia?

162   ¿En qué año empezó a trabajar estos terrenos?

Ahora, unas preguntas sobre los cambios que han habido en cuanto a sus terrenos desde que los empezó a trabajar.

163   Desde que empezó a trabajar estos terrenos, ¿cómo ha cambiado...?

		Más	Menos	Igual	NA	NS/NQR
a	El tamaño de sus terrenos	1	2	3	8888	9999
b	El tiempo que invierte en trabajar el campo (incluye tiempo de familia)	1	2	3	8888	9999
c	El dinero que invierte en el campo	1	2	3	8888	9999
d	La cantidad que produce cada hectárea	1	2	3	8888	9999

164   Por lo general, ¿diría usted que se está volviendo más difícil sacar comida y dinero de su campo?
165   (En caso de "sí":) ¿A qué se debe esto? (NO LEA LAS RESPUESTAS. MARQUE TODAS LAS QUE APLIQUEN.)

       1 Migración de mano de obra
       2 Sequía
       3 Mayor costo de producción

161

4 Falta de mano de obra
5 Menor precio de producto agrícola
6 Falta de apoyo de las autoridades federales o estatales
7 Falta de apoyo de las autoridades municipales, en Tunkás
8 Otro (especifique) _____

166   ¿Usted depende exclusivamente de la lluvia para regar la cosecha?

167   *(En caso de "sí":)* ¿La falta de agua causa problemas para su cosecha?

168   ¿Ha intentado reemplazar la lluvia con otros métodos de riego?

169   ¿Usted quisiera invertir en un sistema colectivo de riego?

170   ¿Estaría dispuesto/a a pagar por un sistema de riego?

171   En los últimos 10 años, ¿ha bajado la cantidad de tiempo que deja descansar la tierra entre cosechas?

172   Si tuviera la posibilidad, ¿dejaría de trabajar en el campo?

173   ¿Usted o algún miembro de su hogar ha usado lo que gana del campo para ayudar a algún miembro de su familia a viajar a otra parte de México o a los Estados Unidos?

        1 Sí, a México
        2 Sí, a Estados Unidos
        3 Sí, a México y Estados Unidos
        4 No

174   *(En caso de "sí":)* ¿Cuántas veces hizo esto?

175   ¿Usted jamás ha vendido algún terreno? (LEA LAS RESPUESTAS.)

        1 Sí, ha vendido
        2 Sí, ha alquilado
        3 No tiene tierra que se pueda vender
        4 No ha vendido

176   ¿Para qué usó este dinero?
177   ¿Cree que le daría una ventaja a su familia vender su tierra?

178   *(En caso de "sí":)* ¿Para qué?
        (MARQUE TODAS LAS QUE APLIQUEN.)

        1 Migrar
        2 Comprar una casa
        3 Construir una casa
        4 Pagar una enfermedad
        5 Pagar la educación
        6 Comprar maquinaria
        7 Otro

179   ¿Usted ha cedido su derecho a otra persona por necesidad?

180 Por la migración de otros tunkaseños, ¿se ha hecho más fácil tener terrenos para trabajar en Tunkás?

EDUCACIÓN

Ahora quisiera preguntarle sobre sus experiencias y opiniones acerca de la educación.

181 ¿Alguien en su familia participa en el programa Prospera (antes Oportunidades)? (LEA LAS OPCIONES.)

>1 Sí
>2 No
>3 Antes participaba, ahora no

182 ¿Por qué dejó de participar?

183 En su opinión ¿piensa que el plan de estudios de la(s) preparatoria(s) en su comunidad prepara a los estudiantes para trabajar en...? (LEA LAS OPCIONES. MARQUE TODAS LAS QUE APLIQUEN.)

>1 En la agricultura
>2 En algún oficio que pague igual o más que la agricultura
>3 Ninguno

184 En su opinión, ¿el plan de estudios de la(s) preparatoria(s) en su comunidad prepara a los estudiantes para seguir adelante con los estudios universitarios?

185 ¿Cuáles son algunos obstáculos para terminar la preparatoria en México? (MARQUE TODAS LAS QUE APLIQUEN.)
>1 El costo
>2 Ayudar con trabajo doméstico
>3 Necesidad de trabajar
>4 Calidad de escuelas
>5 Transporte
>6 Falta de diversidad en materias
>7 Falta de ánimo/interés
>8 Discriminación
>9 Falta de preparación
>10 Enfermedad o discapacidad
>11 Planes de familia
>12 Otro (especifique) _____

186 De los obstáculos que Ud. menciono (en la pregunta anterior), ¿cuál sería el *mayor* obstáculo?

187 ¿Cuáles son algunos obstáculos para ingresar a la universidad en México?

188 De los obstáculos que Ud. menciono (en la pregunta anterior), ¿cuál sería el *mayor* obstáculo?

189 ¿Cuales son algunos obstáculos para terminar la universidad en México? (MARQUE TODAS LAS QUE APLIQUEN.)

1 Falta de ánimo/interés
2 El costo
3 Ayudar con trabajo domestico
4 Necesidad de trabajar
5 Transporte
6 Obligaciones familiares
7 Falta de preparación para los estudios universitarios
8 Enfermedad o discapacidad
9 Discriminación
10 Otro (especifique) _____
11 No hay obstáculos

190 De los obstáculos que Ud. menciono (en la pregunta anterior), ¿cuál sería el *mayor* obstáculo?

191 ¿Qué tan importantes son las clases de agricultura para que los jóvenes de hoy encuentren un trabajo? (LEA LAS OPCIONES.)

1 Muy importantes
2 Algo importantes
3 Poco importantes
4 Nada importantes

> ➢ PREGUNTE A TODOS LOS QUE VIVEN EN LOS EEUU.

---

192 ¿Cuáles son algunos obstáculos para terminar la preparatoria en EEUU? **(MARQUE TODAS LAS QUE APLIQUEN.)**

1 El costo
2 Ayudar con trabajo domestico
3 Necesidad de trabajar
4 Calidad de escuelas
5 Transporte
6 Falta de diversidad en materias
7 Falta de ánimo/interés
8 Discriminación
9 Falta de preparación
10 Enfermedad o discapacidad
11 Planes de familia
12 Estatus migratorio
13 Capacidad limitada con el inglés
14 Otro (especifique) _____

193 De los obstáculos que Ud. menciono (en la pregunta anterior), ¿cuál sería el *mayor* obstáculo?

194 ¿Cuáles son algunos obstáculos para ingresar a la universidad en EEUU? (MARQUE TODAS LAS QUE APLIQUEN.)

1 El costo
2 Ayudar con trabajo domestico
3 Necesidad de trabajar
4 Transporte
5 Obligaciones familiares

164

6 Falta de preparación para los estudios universitarios
7 Enfermedad o discapacidad
8 Falta de ánimo/interés
9 Discriminación
10 Falta de acceso a información sobre el proceso de admisión y ayuda financiera
11 Estatus migratorio
12 Capacidad limitada con el inglés
13 Importancia de quedarse cerca de la familia
14 Otro (especifique) _____

195   De los obstáculos que Ud. menciono (en la pregunta anterior), ¿cuál sería el *mayor* obstáculo?

196   ¿Cuales son algunos obstáculos para terminar a la universidad en EEUU?

197   De los obstáculos que Ud. mencionó (en la pregunta anterior), ¿cuál sería el *mayor* obstáculo?

➤ PREGUNTE A TODOS.

198   ¿Actualmente Ud. está en la escuela?

199   *(En caso de "no":)* ¿Salió de la primaria antes de graduarse?

200   ¿Salió de la secundaria antes de graduarse?

201   ¿Salió de la preparatoria antes de graduarse?

202   ¿Salió de la universidad antes de graduarse?

203   ¿Por qué salió de la escuela?
(MARQUE LA RAZÓN MÁS IMPORTANTE.)

1 El costo
2 Para trabajar por decisión propia
3 Satisfecho con el nivel aprobado
4 Para trabajar y aportar para mantenimiento de familia
5 Migración internacional
6 Migración interna
7 No había maestros o escuela para próximo nivel
8 No había cupo para próximo nivel
9 Capacidad limitada con el inglés
10 Para casarse
11 Planes familiares
12 Trabajo domestico
13 Falta de ánimo/interés
14 Por enfermedad o discapacidad
15 Estatus migratorio
16 No enseñaron lo que quisiera
17 Otro (especifique) _____

204   ¿Por qué no entró en el próximo nivel de la escuela?

205   Pensando en la escuela a la que usted asiste actualmente o la últimaescuela a la que usted asistió, ¿Usted diría que … de esta escuela son muy buenas, buenas, malas o muy malas?

		Muy Buenas	Buenas	Malas	Muy Malas	NA	NS/NQR
a	Las instalaciones	1	2	3	4	8888	9999
b	Las materias	1	2	3	4	8888	9999
c	La capacidad de los maestros	1	2	3	4	8888	9999
d	La regularidad de las clases	1	2	3	4	8888	9999
e	La seguridad de los niños	1	2	3	4	8888	9999

206   Ahora vamos a hablar sobre el interés de sus padres o tutores en los estudios de usted. Por favor indique la frecuencia con la cual sus padres o tutores hacen/hacían lo siguiente (mientras estudiaba).

		A veces	Nunca o casi nunca	NA	NS/NQR
a	Platican/platicaban con Ud. sobre la tarea	1	2	8888	9999
b	Platican/platicaban con Ud. sobre estudiar en una universidad	1	2	8888	9999
c	Preguntan/preguntaban sobre notas/calificaciones	1	2	8888	9999
d	Platican/platicaban con sus maestros sobre su progreso	1	2	8888	9999
e	Le obligan/ obligaban a ir a la escuela	1	2	8888	9999
f	Asisten/asistían a eventos organizados por la escuela	1	2	8888	9999

Ahora vamos a hablar acerca de sus maestros en su escuela/ en la última escuela a la que asistió. Dígame qué tan de acuerdo está con las siguientes frases.

207   "(Cuando yo era estudiante,) los maestros de mi escuela se interesan/interesaron en mi trabajo en la escuela."
(LEA LAS OPCIONES.)

        1 Muy de acuerdo
        2 Algo de acuerdo
        3 Poco de acuerdo
        4 Nada de acuerdo

208   "(Cuando yo era estudiante,) mis maestros esperan/esperaban que yo termine/terminara la preparatoria. (LEA LAS OPCIONES.)

        1 Muy de acuerdo
        2 Algo de acuerdo
        3 Poco de acuerdo
        4 Nada de acuerdo

209   "(Cuando yo era estudiante,) mis maestros me hablan/hablaban a menudo sobre estudiar en la universidad. (LEA LAS OPCIONES.)

        1 Muy de acuerdo
        2 Algo de acuerdo
        3 Poco de acuerdo
        4 Nada de acuerdo

210   "(Cuando yo era estudiante,) mis maestros esperan/esperaban que yo logre/lograra una carrera universitaria." (LEA LAS OPCIONES.)

        1 Muy de acuerdo
        2 Algo de acuerdo
        3 Poco de acuerdo
        4 Nada de acuerdo

➤ **PREGUNTE A TODOS.**

Ahora quiero preguntarle más sobre el uso de idiomas en su vida cotidiana.

211   ¿Qué idioma habla con *sus padres* la mayoría del tiempo?
(LEA LAS OPCIONES.)

        1 Inglés
        2 Español
        3 Maya
        4 Otro

212   ¿Qué idioma habla con *sus hermanos* la mayoría del tiempo?
(LEA LAS OPCIONES.)

        1 Inglés

2 Español
3 Maya
4 Otro

213   ¿Qué idioma habla con *sus amigos* la mayoría del tiempo?
       (LEA LAS OPCIONES.)

              1 Inglés
              2 Español
              3 Maya
              4 Otro

MIGRACIÓN Y VIDA FAMILIAR

Para terminar le voy a hacer algunas preguntas sobre la familia y los adolescentes.

214   De la lista que le voy a leer, ¿qué situaciones aplican, la mayoría del tiempo, para un adolescente que vive en Tunkás y que su padre vive y trabaja en los Estados Unidos? (LEA CADA OPCIÓN E INDIQUE SÍ O NO.)

		Sí	No	NA	NS/NQR
A	Se siente abandonado	1	2	8888	9999
B	Se siente diferente a los demás	1	2	8888	9999
C	Sus compañeros se burlan de él o de ella en la escuela	1	2	8888	9999
D	Se burlan de él/ella afuera de la escuela	1	2	8888	9999
E	Le va mal en la escuela	1	2	8888	9999
F	Está descuidado	1	2	8888	9999

215   ¿Cuándo es más difícil disciplinar a los adolescentes?
       (LEA LAS OPCIONES.)
              1 Cuando los adolescentes viven en Tunkás
              2 Cuando los adolescentes viven en Estados Unidos
              3 Cuando los adolescentes viven en Quintana Roo (u otras partes
                    de la Península de Yucatán)
              4 Es igual, no importa donde vivan

Ahora le voy a hacer unas preguntas sobre el uso de alcohol y otras sustancias entre adolescentes.

216   Voy a leer una lista de ocasiones en las que puede haber oportunidad para que los adolescentes tomen alcohol. En su opinión, ¿qué tan frecuente es que los adolescentes de acá (Tunkás/Estados Unidos) tomen alcohol en estas situaciones?
       (LEER TODAS Y MARCAR LAS QUE APLIQUEN.)

	Nunca o casi nunca	A veces	Muy seguido	NA	NS/ NQR

a	Cuando están sin vigilancia en sus casas	1	2	3	8888	9999
b	Cuando van a la cancha o campo de juego	1	2	3	8888	9999
c	Cuando hay bailes, conciertos, tocadas, luz y sonido, etc.	1	2	3	8888	9999
d	Durante la fiesta del pueblo/kermeses	1	2	3	8888	9999
e	Saliendo de la escuela con sus compañeros	1	2	3	8888	9999
f	Durante el fin de semana, en los días de descanso	1	2	3	8888	9999

217   ¿Cómo es que los adolescentes de acá (Tunkás/Estados Unidos) consiguen bebidas alcohólicas?
(LEA LAS OPCIONES. MARQUE TODAS LAS QUE APLIQUEN.)

1 Ellos mismos las compran
2 Sus amigos se las dan
3 Un familiar se las da
4 Otro

218   Cuando migra un padre, ¿es más probable que un adolescente que vive en Tunkás comience a tomar alcohol o que tome más?

1 Sí, es más probable que comience a tomar o que tome más
2 No, no influye para que comience a tomar o que tome más

219   De los siguientes lugares que le voy a leer, ¿dónde es *más fácil* para los adolescentes varones conseguir alcohol? (LEA LAS OPCIONES.)

1 Tunkás
2 Quintana Roo (u otras partes de la Península de Yucatán)
3 Estados Unidos

220   ¿Y para las adolescentes mujeres, ¿dónde es más fácil conseguir alcohol? (LEA LAS OPCIONES.)

1 Tunkás
2 Quintana Roo (u otras partes de la Península de Yucatán)
3 Estados Unidos

221   De la siguiente lista, ¿qué hace que los adolescentes no se metan en problemas de alcohol? (LEA CADA OPCIÓN E INDIQUE SÍ O NO.)

		Sí	No	NA	NS/NQR
a	Que es su forma o modo de ser	1	2	8888	9999
b	Que la familia los vigila	1	2	8888	9999
c	Que no tienen malas amistades o malos compañeros	1	2	8888	9999
d	Que las autoridades del pueblo/ciudad están pendientes	1	2	8888	9999

Y pensando en *las drogas* como marihuana, cocaína, pastillas, drogas no recetables:

222   Le voy a leer una lista de ocasiones en las que puede haber oportunidad para que los adolescentes consuman drogas. En su opinión, ¿qué tan frecuente es que los adolescentes de acá (Tunkás/Estados Unidos) consuman drogas en estas situaciones?
(LEER TODAS Y MARCAR LAS QUE APLIQUEN.)

		Nunca o casi nunca	A veces	Muy seguido	NA	NS/ NQR
a	Cuando están sin vigilancia en sus casas	1	2	3	8888	9999
b	Cuando van a la cancha o campo de juego	1	2	3	8888	9999
c	Cuando hay bailes, conciertos, tocadas, luz y sonido, etc.	1	2	3	8888	9999
d	Durante la fiesta del pueblo/kermeses	1	2	3	8888	9999
e	Saliendo de la escuela con sus compañeros	1	2	3	8888	9999
f	Durante el fin de semana, en los días de descanso	1	2	3	8888	9999

223   ¿Cómo es que los jóvenes de acá (Tunkás/Estados Unidos) consiguen drogas?
(LEA LAS OPCIONES. MARQUE TODAS LAS QUE APLIQUEN.)

1 Ellos mismos las compran
2 Sus amigos se las dan

3 Un familiar se las da
4 Otro

224   Cuando migra un padre, ¿es más probable que un adolescente que vive en
       Tunkás comience a usar drogas o que consuma más?

       1 Sí, es más probable que comience a consumir o que consuma más
       2 No, no influye para que comience a consumir o que consuma más

225   De la siguiente lista, ¿dónde es más fácil para los adolescentes VARONES
       conseguir drogas? (LEA LAS OPCIONES.)

       1 Tunkás
       2 Quintana Roo (u otras partes de la Península de
       Yucatán)
       3 Estados Unidos

226   ¿Y para las adolescentes mujeres, ¿dónde es más fácil conseguirlas? (LEA LAS
       OPCIONES.)

       1 Tunkás
       2 Quintana Roo (u otras partes de la Península de
       Yucatán)
       3 Estados Unidos

227   ¿Cuándo cree que los jóvenes de Tunkás se pueden echar a perder más? (LEA
       LAS OPCIONES.)

       1 Cuando su padre está en los Estados Unidos
       2 Cuando su padre está en Quintana Roo (u otras partes de la
       Península de Yucatán)
       3 Cuando su padre está en Tunkás
       4 Es igual, no depende de donde viva el padre

228   ¿Qué hace que los jóvenes no se metan en problemas de drogas?
       (LEA CADA OPCIÓN E INDIQUE SÍ O NO.)

		Sí	No	NA	NS/NQR
a	Que es su forma o modo de ser	1	2	8888	9999
b	Que la familia los vigila	1	2	8888	9999
c	Que no tienen malas amistades o malos compañeros	1	2	8888	9999
d	Que las autoridades del pueblo/ciudad están pendientes	1	2	8888	9999

TERMINACIÓN DE ENTREVISTA

Nos gustaría conocer a los Tunkaseños que viven en los Estados Unidos, no solamente la gente que se encuentra en Tunkás durante nuestra visita. ¿Me puede decir cómo podemos ponernos en contacto con familiares o amigos suyos que actualmente viven en EEUU? Esperamos visitarlos cuando regresemos a California.

Ya terminamos. Muchísimas gracias por su tiempo y por su ayuda con nuestro estudio.